I0623391

LOOK UP!

A Wild & Screen Freed Roadmap to Enjoying Travel with Kids

JENNA LEE DILLON

LOOK UP! A Wild & Screen Freed Roadmap to Enjoying Travel with Kids

©2024 Jenna Lee Dillon. All Rights Reserved.

Paperback ISBN: 979-8-9907269-0-1
Ebook ISBN: 979-8-9907269-1-8

Library of Congress Control Number: 2024909766

Edited by Terra Rose Ganem-Sorrell
Cover Design & Interior Layout by Ronda Taylor, HeartWorkCreative.com

Published by Choose a Better You, LLC
Sheridan, Wyoming

Dedication

To LP, this book exists because of you. My Wildflower, thank you for being an extraordinary travel companion and my all-around favorite human. I love you the mostest.

To all my fellow parents—the ones I get to parent alongside and all those I'll never meet—for embracing the adventure of parenthood with audacious love and bravery. You inspire me.

To those who held me, fed me, nourished my heart, listened to my doubts, or sweated over this book as much as me. You know who you are. Thank you times a million.

Contents

CHAPTER 1

Your Passport to Magic has Arrived

F OR SOMEONE WHO FLIES AN AVERAGE OF ONCE A MONTH, I DON'T spend much time in terminals. Usually, my boarding experience includes a bedraggled sprint through the airport (often carrying my daughter, LP) that leaves me panting in front of the gate agent, sweat streaming down my back as I fumble through my phone trying to find my e-ticket while Southwest passengers step around me to board.

This time, LP and I were early for our flight. We actually *meandered* through the airport. Neither of us were accustomed to all that free time. Then, I caught sight of something at the end of the terminal.

Golden-hour light streamed through a massive floor-to-ceiling window where a small group of adults and children gathered. As LP and I approached, the reason for the crowd of children came into view. They were playing a giant Connect 4 game. Parents stood around them, some on their phones, some watching planes out the window, several observing the kids.

The children were doing what children do.

Without even exchanging names, the invitation to play was offered. A scruffy haired toddler handed a round, red Connect 4 coin roughly the size of his face to my daughter. LP stood on tiptoes, the two blonde travel buns atop of her head barely clearing the third row of the game, to slide the coin into a top slot. It fell down with a plastic-on-plastic thunk, making a red row of four.

Nobody seemed to know the game was won; clearly, the rules were not in play. Instead, it was playground protocol where collaboration and the energy of creation are how everyone wins. The children worked to fill each slot with a coin, bigger kids lifting up younger siblings to reach.

When one lucky child got to pull the lever releasing all the coins to the floor in a satisfying clatter, the children clapped and started over. Parents exchanged smiles, and I'm pretty sure I wasn't the only adult who secretly wanted to be the lever-puller.

The kids played. I chatted with several parents. When our flight was called, LP and I departed with waves and goodbyes to the other families.

There was a togetherness in the terminal that day. There was a bond forged in the simplicity of child's play beneath rays of Colorado sunshine. There, amidst the harried energy of people on the go, was a pause and presence in the name of childhood and simple joy.

It's a treasure of travel to share a passing moment with strangers you'll never meet again and let it open your heart. These little nuggets of gold are common when we make ourselves available to them by being present in the moment. But I might have missed out on them if not for an important conversation I'll share in Chapter 3. First, let's chat about why you're here reading this book.

The Screen Freed Travel Dream

Picture this for your next trip …

You arrive at your destination feeling exhilarated and ready for adventure instead of drained.

How is this possible?

During travel, your child(ren) didn't ask for screen time or easily accepted your answer of "not at this time."

You and your child(ren) engaged one another and made memories. You watched the adventure unfold through the wonder in their eyes.

You're not stressed because your phone battery was devoured by *Cocomelon* on the flight.

You're not fumbling for the nearest plug-in when you land because you're 1% of iPad battery life away from a major meltdown.

Your kid(s) often self-entertained during transit and the duration of travel.

You know there are more trips down the road. Instead of the 10-pound weight you used to feel in your stomach about pending travel, you feel confident. You know you and your family can handle whatever comes.

Upon arriving back home, your child asks with excitement, "When can we do that again?!"

All of this is entirely possible.

Look Up! is meant to inspire families to travel better. Better can't be quantified by the hours of screen time or number of devices.

Better can only be felt by you and your family. Better feels like less fear and stress and more groundedness. Better feels like more fun and ease and less stomach-clenching anxiety. Better feels like the warmth of a shared smile and eye contact, the snuggle of a small body heavy with sleep in your arms, and the glow of adventure on your child's face as they recount their travel stories. Better is a mindset that you can cultivate no matter how the actual travel turns out.

Together, we will travel better with our families.

Travel: The Pressure Cooker Effect

After my daughter was born, I quickly learned that travel was going to look very different from my pre-kid days. I was still married when my infant daughter, her father, and I road tripped from Colorado to Arizona. It is a 14-hour drive in normal circumstances. With a baby, we broke it into two days. The drive felt never-ending with seemingly countless stops for feeding and diaper changes.

Early flights with LP as a lap child entailed me being a one-woman playground while trying to contain her in the allotted 17.5 inches of seat space. Somewhere in the archives of my Instagram stories is a selfie of LP sleeping on my chest after a particularly raucous trip with a tongue-in-cheek caption that reads, "And the entire flight rejoices."

Reality check...

Travel is a pressure cooker. It takes whatever challenges we have in normal day-to-day life and boils them faster.

Have a toddler in a flailing fit phase? Drinking from those spill-prone airline cups will be fun! (Not!) If you've ever tried to wipe up a spilled beverage with airline napkins, you know those useless squares are composed of something far weaker than tissue paper.

Taking a road trip during the potty training phase? This is equivalent to American Ninja Warrior training. If you can cut across three lanes of traffic to the nearest off-ramp, unbuckle a safety seat, remove your child, and de-pant them faster than their bladder can give out, you are *indeed* an athlete.

Your preschooler is struggling with separation anxiety? Walking three feet away from you through the metal detector, while an unsympathetic TSA agent demands, "Only one person at a time!" will be like asking her to fly to the moon without you.

I've experienced all of the above and more. As of this writing, LP and I have been on 54 domestic flights, 11 international flights, and 51 road trips. I'm a single mom, so most of those trips have been just the two of us.

During all those adventures, I have chosen (some people might say *like a crazy person*) not to give my daughter screen time. The gifts of this choice are so delicious.

So when I say that it can be done, I know firsthand it can. We just have to equip *you* to believe it's possible for your family too.

It's been challenging at times. Most times, though, it's been way easier than I ever expected. Fear of how hard it might be stops a lot of people from considering traveling with screen freedom. I'm here to show you all the ways to make it easier! (Cue feelings of relief.)

More than anything, I hope you use this book as a guide to parenting and traveling with more intention. I hope you see that less screen time is really an invitation to more of what you want—presence in the moment, a deep connection with your kids, a whole slew of critical life skills, and a lifetime of memories that you created together.

This Book Has Your Back

Travel contains countless opportunities for magic. This kind of magic waits for people who step out of the heads down, ho-hum of everyday life, for those who dare to explore the world. This magic hovers around travelers, waiting for them to *Look Up!*

You picked up this book because you want your family to experience that magic. You want your kids to travel and explore. You, understandably, want to get the most out of the time and money you've invested in the trip. You want to create lifelong memories with your children, whether from an international adventure or a two-hour road trip to a state park.

But we no longer live in a society that embraces the magic—or the discomfort—of adventure.

We live in a society that has made it easy (and acceptable) to numb reality, so we can sidestep potential pain, boredom, discomfort, or conflict.

Well I have some bad news for you … you can't numb the "bad" stuff without missing out on the good stuff.

I know you don't want your kids to miss the magic of seeing a new place for the first time, of interacting with people outside their norm, of tasting unfamiliar foods and delving into unfamiliar experiences, of discovering the language of the world in order to communicate with someone in a foreign country, of spotting an elk out the window as the car trundles up the mountain, of seeing the sun rise and fill the camping tent with golden light, and of being able to get lost in the wilds of their own imaginations.

I know you don't want numbed out kids, because we're already learning from Generation Z what that leads to (it's *not* pretty).

Yet, society tells us it's easy to have quiet, compliant kids. There's actually a button you can press that will turn them into lap-staring automaton children who are seen but not heard. It's not a button on their body—it's on the tablet. Tada! The iPad easy button!

I'm *always* suspicious when an advertisement tells me they can take a complex process and make it easy. Some experiences *can* be simplified but aren't meant to be easy.

In the case of parenting, there may not be an infomercial host hollering at us "we've made it easy for you" like a circus barker, but we're definitely getting the message from society that we can and should outsource to the iPad.

This book is about doing it differently. This book is about reducing or completely eliminating screen time during travel with your children. My goal by the end of this book is that you'll not only be convinced of the value of such a feat, you'll feel really equipped and empowered to do it. Most importantly, you'll know that what is on the other side of less screen time is more of what you want.

In the following chapters, we are going to explore:

- How to sidestep the pressure society puts on parents and instead choose your own path
- The wild (and unexpected) gifts of traveling with children
- Why screen time typically increases during travel, what this costs us, and exactly what to do about it
- How to say no to a society that tells us we are not capable of parenting without screen dependence and rediscover that you are absolutely capable enough
- How to be your "best self" parent during travel (and at home too!)
- What you and your child actually need to enjoy traveling together (get ready to be surprised!)
- The most extraordinary gift you can give your child (without doing anything at all!)
- What to pack and how to maximize the fun factor while in route
- Super effective resets for the nervous system approved by the whole family
- The one question you must have in your back pocket
- Tools and conversation starters for your Screen Freed lifestyle

We'll go over helpful mindset tools that not only support traveling screen freed with kids but getting through the day-to-day challenges of being a parent.

I'll share my screen freed travel hacks. Some were ... shall we say ... learned via trial and error (so much error). I wrote this to save you the trouble of learning them yourself.

I'll also share stories from our travels, including the less-than-ideal ones. This way, you know I'm a human parent just like you, not some robot with a perfect robot child who made traveling without screens super easy.

I'll *never* ask you to do anything that I haven't done. And I won't shy away from this fact:

In choosing to cut back or wipe out screen time during travel, you *are* choosing the harder path (at least in the short term).

Ah but, my friend, you are also choosing the *magic*.

A Good Time or a Good Story

I was once told an adventure should either result in a good time or a good story.

Boy, do I have some good … stories.

We've dealt with all sorts of travel mishaps and obstacles as we adventured together from her infancy to kindergarten. To name a few: a two-hour delay on the tarmac in Phoenix, Arizona without the benefit of air conditioning, a 14-hour road trip during early COVID days in which 3-year-old LP and I did all potty breaks outside to avoid exposure, and finding out on a cross-Atlantic flight that mine is one of the small percentage of babies who get wound up instead of drowsy on Benadryl. What was challenging in the moment at least made for a few good stories.

Luckily, we've had good times too.

The pressure cooker metaphor applies to all the wonderful moments as much as the challenges. Travel has a way of searing the little golden moments into our memories. It enables us to look beyond the daily clutter of life to see the extraordinary, chaotic, wonderful adventure we chose when we became parents.

Being present and mostly off my device has enabled me to watch LP immerse herself in travel. I wouldn't trade these memories for anything: my girl's dimpled grin as she watches the airplane's "wing brakes" unfold, the thrill of seeing a fox trot across a dusk-dimmed field as we drive by, the simple joy of seeing a loved one pull up to the curb to collect us after a long flight, the delight as she tells every single flight attendant, "We're flying to Phoenix to see my great grandparents. They're really old but still lots of fun," her comforting words to our seatmate who is struggling with flight anxiety, and the warmth of her hand in mine as we cross an unfamiliar street in a new city full of the promise of adventure.

What memories are waiting for your family to create?

Through all those screen freed flights, road trips, hotels, campouts, AirBNBs, ferries, buses, and trains, I've learned a lot. Just like mine has been, your travel journey will be fulfilling, confronting, fun, exhausting, exciting; you name it, you will taste it from the buffet of emotions.

Screen freed travel is so much easier for me now after all I've learned. Isn't it great that you have this book so you don't have to learn the hard way like I did?

Whether you use the strategies in this book to travel entirely screen-free or to reduce your family's dependence on devices while traveling, you are already on a journey to becoming screen freed. You want to do something different than you have been doing or different from how the majority of folks approach screens and travel. By picking up this book, you have begun.

CHAPTER 2

How to Find Your Path and Make the Most of *Look Up!*

You and I, We're Fellow Adventurers ...

W ELL, ACTUALLY IT'S MORE ACCURATE TO SAY IN THIS BOOK, I'M less your fellow adventurer and more a full-service tour guide. I've done the planning and heavy lifting, so that you can venture bravely where you've never gone before.

Some of the pieces in this book may surprise you as the tried and true way to get to screen freedom. I'm here to be your insider adventure guide. My mission is to ensure you have exactly what you need and give you a perspective most people won't.

If you're like me, you loved travel long before you had kids. You didn't really care where you were going as long as you were going somewhere. You, too, craved the unfamiliar and the novelty of travel and reveled in the possibility of who you might choose to be in a new place.

Or maybe you're *not* like me, and travel feels like a lot of planning and work. Despite that, you have dreams of taking your kids on trips to see more of the world.

Maybe you have avoided traveling with kids thus far because you think it will be a disaster, but you really want to try it.

All perspectives are welcome. It doesn't matter if you live for travel, tolerate it as a means to an end, or simply hope to do it one day, this is true for you:

You can travel with your kids *and* you can do it while being heads up to the world, present in the moment, and helping your kids do the same.

Whether you want to be entirely screen-free during travel, or you seek to reduce your family's screen time, your effectiveness will come from your mindset, *not* from how your family currently uses technology or has used it in the past. In short, it doesn't matter where you're coming from. If you can answer yes to the following questions, this book is for you:

Do you want to limit dependence on devices while traveling?

Are you willing to examine your thoughts and reactions to what we talk about in this book?

Will you be honest with yourself?

Do you want healthy parenting strategies that you can use during and outside of travel to be more free, more present, more comfortable with the unknown, and more secure in who you are as a caregiver?

If you said yes to those questions—even if it was a hesitant yes with an invisible question mark—then let's get started. All you need is that willingness and some free time to read. (And if you don't have a lot of free time, don't worry; that's one of the things we're going to work on getting more of for you in this book!)

What This Journey Is Not

This book is not a set of rules to follow, but it is a roadmap you can trust.

This book is not a reprimand for parents. It doesn't matter if you've given gobs of screen time and will allow it in the future or whether you live in a tech-free household deep in the woods. I'm writing this to give you resources. No judgment here. In fact, after reading this book, you will have more tools to better ignore the judgment of others and identify and change habits of self-judgment.

This book is not a secret sauce that will make travel with kids easy breezy every time. I wish, my fellow parent, that there was a simple instruction manual I could print off for you that would make travel with children completely effortless. Then I would be rich, and you and all the other readers would be thrilled.

But we're parents. We know that those who try to sell us the "just do these three things and all your parenting woes will disappear" are selling snake oil. Yes, there are techniques that work really well, except for the times they don't. Human beings are not appliances. We are not identical piles of metal churned out on an assembly line. We are ever-changing, complex beings of mystery, unknown sometimes even to ourselves. The best work we can do is equal parts curiosity—about ourselves and our children and why we do what we do—and acceptance.

How to Prepare for Our Adventure

Step One:

Be raising or spending time with children you love.

Throughout these pages, I will mostly use the term "parent" to reference you, the reader. That's for ease of communication, not to exclude the incredible people out there who are not parents but *are* caregivers. When you read "parent," please envision yourself in the title that feels best for you and know I am most certainly speaking to you as a child's loved one.

Step Two:

Trust yourself. (If you don't have that muscle yet, we'll build it together in the mindset chapter.)

We often exist in a state of survival as parents. I find myself wanting someone in a comfortingly short Instagram video to tell me what to do, cite a study that sounds legit, and make it convincing enough that my nervous system accepts their solution. Anyone else?

But the reality is we don't *need* anyone else to tell us how to be parents to our children. This book isn't about that. This book is about supporting you, sharing my experiences (for entertainment, solidarity, and learning), and offering tools. I'll give you strategies and trust you to use them in the way that fits your one-of-a-kind family.

Step Three:

Begin to observe the children around you.

You have the ability to observe the effects of screens on kids without needing to read any studies or agree with any doctrines or be a "this or that" branded parent.

Look around you. Watch kids who are playing make believe at the park, and watch kids who are staring at a screen. Who looks lit up and energized? Who is making eye contact with other humans, and who is alone in a digital world? Who is quiet and who is loud? Who is moving their body and who is still? Who is using their imagination and who is consuming the product of someone else's imagination?

I can throw a bunch of scary statistics at you. I can cite studies and experts who will tell you the negative effects of screen time on children *and* adults. I could also provide you with examples of all the goodness technology has enabled in the world. As a longtime marketer, I know either side of a story can be argued effectively.

But that would be trying to convince you of something for my reasons. I want you to find your own. Likely, you've already considered that less screen time will have positive effects on everyone in your family. How do I know? You're reading this book.

Whatever observations you make, it's up to you to decide what you want for your family. If it's to analyze, understand, and consciously choose the role screens play in your child's life, specifically while traveling, I can help you.

■ Step Four:

Show up with all your feelings doing whatever feeling-y thing they want to do.

We will cover serious topics, though I will be lighthearted whenever possible. Together, we will lean into the chaos that is rearing kids in the modern world: parenting with less community, less support, higher expectations, and more complexity than ever. Welcome to the madness…

"But I don't want to go among mad people," Alice remarked.
"Oh, you can't help that," said the Cat. "We're all mad here. I'm mad. You're mad."
"How do you know I'm mad?" said Alice.
"You must be," said the Cat, "or you wouldn't have come here."

—LEWIS CARROLL, *ALICE IN WONDERLAND*

As you read along, let yourself laugh or cry if it feels right. Or do both at once. I get it. You've come here seeking shared understanding and growth. Growth always leads to a lot of feelings, some uncomfortable. There's room for them here. There's room for all of your parts here.

In fact, I'll ask you to pay attention to the thoughts and feelings that come up for you as you read. This kind of attuning to yourself is a great way to learn about what is unconsciously driving your choices and actions. From that point, you can avoid being reactive and can be intentional and present.

I'll end the sections that address mindset with a Check In. These open-ended questions are opportunities for you to feel into your truth, multilayered and complex as it will likely be. They offer you a chance to get to know yourself better so you can navigate the wild challenge of being a human being (with your own needs) and a parent simultaneously. It may help to journal your responses. If these sections feel too much like homework, skip them. You can always come back to them later.

▩ Step Five:

Have you ever heard this saying? "You can go faster alone, but you can go farther together." I love it.

Sometimes I choose to go faster alone, especially when I'm pioneering a new idea. But then I do my best to rally others to go with me, because it's more effective and more fun to move together. That's why I created the Facebook group *Wild and Screen Free Travel Families*. It's a place for folks like us to exchange tips and ideas, celebrate travel wins, engage in thoughtful conversations, and find much-needed community. Feel free to join by searching for the group by name on Facebook or scanning the QR code below; I'd love to meet you (virtually) there!

CHAPTER 3

How It All Started

G LASSES CLINKED AND CONVERSATION BUZZED AROUND US AT THE cocktail party. A friend I hadn't seen in several years approached me. Within minutes, she was asking when I planned to have children (as people do basically the second your wedding is over).

I said, "I don't want to stop traveling." That wasn't really an answer to her question but it was a response to my fear: *What if when I have a kid I have to stop doing the thing I love most?*

She gave a knowing smile and launched into a story about her recent travels. She has four children and had just taken them on a trip to Cuba. She and the children had flown out a month before her husband. As the solo parent, she had navigated the international flight and the long stay with distant in-laws in a foreign country. She described in an easygoing voice the adventures she and her children had and what they had learned in the foreign country. As her story unfolded, it dawned on me that I didn't *have* to stop or significantly reduce my traveling when I became a mother.

She concluded, "It'll look different, but you must bring them along. Don't change something that is fundamental to who you are, because don't you want it to be fundamental to who your children are too?"

Cue me nodding vigorously and feeling encouraged.

But her story did more than inspire me. It revealed the trap I was already falling into—and I wasn't even a parent yet!

This is a summary of the messages I was getting from society about parenthood—and especially motherhood:

Parenthood is a martyrdom. Parenthood meant giving up the things I love most, and devoting my entire life to the children. My dreams, hobbies, and recreation should be squeezed into the leftover scraps of time (or ignored entirely). Top-notch parenting meant putting the children and their preferences, playdates, and 24/7 entertainment above all else.

If it sounds absurd to read it so plainly stated, it's because this type of societal programming is usually more subtle. It's cleverly couched in "mom guilt" and "do you even dad?" It's in the side glances parents get when they talk about pursuing ambitions and making time for their recreation. It's the times we've heard parents being judged for taking vacations without their children.

Society's powerful insinuation is that our love for our children is measured by how much we lose ourselves in caring for them.

Until that conversation with my friend, I wasn't getting many messages that an alternative was possible. I wasn't hearing that I could continue to do the things I love and still be a great mom. I wasn't hearing that it might actually be *healthier* for my child to see me engaging in things that brought me joy.

Travel Is My North Star

Every time I board a plane or gas up for a road trip, I nod to the person I was before becoming a mother. Every time we set off on a new adventure, I show past-me that she is still part of present-me. I show myself and my daughter that everyone in our family matters.

It's also become a lesson in bringing my daughter along. It's a reminder that, together, we can navigate new situations and find our place again and again in unfamiliar environments. Our homebase is each other, and we can take that with us anywhere we adventure.

Travel has brought my daughter and I close together. We've forged a bond in the shared excitement and effort of adventuring. I've watched her confidence bloom, and I fully believe it's due in part to the variety of travel experiences she has had.

My confidence has grown too. It's hard to remember the younger me who nearly let society's unempowering messages dim my dreams of traveling and my desire to share it with my future child. I'm grateful to my friend for sharing her story and encouragement.

It's not as if the cultural messaging went away. I still feel the pushback from society and even from people close to me who don't know they're parroting these confining worldviews. The judgment still occurs.

Instead, I developed a bullshit radar system that enables me to swipe aside unhelpful outside opinions like they're a bad match on Hinge. I'll help you develop that super power in the course of this book. With practice, you will be able to ignore outside influences and tune into your desires and beliefs to choose your own path.

Navigating With Your Own Compass

You may have to amend how the process looks, but you do not have to give up on your dreams of travel, with and without your kids. In fact, you do not have to give up on *any* of your dreams when you become a parent. You just have to be flexible with how you achieve them.

For me, the biggest dream is travel. You may have other aspirations—running a long distance race, starting a business, going back to school, reading 50 books in a year, or having a clean house for an entire 24 hours.

Whatever your dream, guard yourself carefully against people, institutions, and influences that would tell you to give it up once you become a parent.

If you need one, let me be your light, like that friend was for me. Let me remind you, it doesn't matter how limited a life anyone else is living. Make up your mind about what matters to you and refuse to accept less. You are here to do the things you dream of! The added benefit—and it's a big one—is that you will model a fulfilled life for your children along the way.

CHAPTER 4

What Is Screen Freedom All About?

Y OU'VE ALREADY SEEN THE PHRASE "SCREEN FREED" IN PREVIOUS chapters. Maybe you thought it was a typo, but it is intentional. I use the terms screen freed and screen-free very differently.

Screen Freed™ is the state of experiencing screen freedom. It is *not* synonymous with screen-free.

Screen-free is a personal choice you may or may not make for your family. For most people, screen-free is a pass/fail grade guaranteed to flood you with righteous pride or lonely shame depending on the day. For perfectionists, it's a dangerous standard with a steep downside.

Screen freedom is the goal of this book, and it's a wish I have for every single person on this planet.

Screen freedom is about being conscious of the choices we make regarding how and why our families uses screens. It's about action based on awareness. It's about knowing the risks and making informed choices. It's about eradicating dependence and replacing it with deliberate choice. Being screen freed requires honesty and a willingness to look deep within ourselves *and* at the messages we're receiving from society.

Like every aspect of parenting, screen freedom makes room for nuance, complexity, and flexibility. You know, the stuff of life with kids?

Screen freed is exactly what the name indicates—it's liberty.

It is possible to be screen-free and *not* screen freed. This is exactly where I found myself about four years ago.

A Little Winnie-the-Pooh Didn't Hurt

It was May of 2020. I was living alone with LP in our family home. We hadn't seen her father since our separation two months earlier. In those two months, my daughter had gone from being a toddler who loved playing independently and only reacted strongly to being separated at school to a toddler who sobbed and chased me if I left the room. She couldn't go to bed without me laying on the floor by her crib. When I didn't, she'd cry for hours before falling asleep. She wailed when I walked away even if she was held by my mom or sister, her two other favorite people in the world.

She was diagnosed with severe separation anxiety. It was hardly a surprise. One parent had suddenly disappeared from her life. Furthermore, she was undoubtedly soaking up some of my fears as I navigated a global pandemic that began a week after I became a single parent.

At this time, LP was still completely screen-free. She didn't watch any TV or interact with smart devices or screens. Although it was a time of tribulation and uncertainty, I had drawn this line in the proverbial parenting sand.

Then one day, I had a virtual meeting scheduled with the judge for my divorce case. I needed to take the meeting in private for two reasons.

One, I didn't want her to see or hear her father on video chat when she hadn't seen him in person. I was concerned this would deepen her confusion and sadness.

Two, my attorney had advised me not to have my daughter with me for the meeting saying it would reflect poorly on me as a parent.

I had no family nearby, and the pandemic had wiped out any daycare options. So I settled for the plan of trying to get her to nap for the meeting.

All morning I did every soothing thing LP loved. We played fetch outside with the dogs. We went on a "chalk walk," decorating our neighborhood's sidewalks with hearts and sunshines like little Banksys of positivity. We'd eaten her favorite foods, and I had rocked her for 45 minutes hoping she'd fall asleep.

But like the emotional lightning rod children often are, she suspected something was afoot and did not succumb to sleep. The meeting was looming. Finally, in desperation, I called the neighbor boy from the only family we had close physical contact with.

LP loved this boy with that infatuation-worship tiny children bestow on bigger children. I hoped the excitement of playing with him would be enough to distract her as I snuck into my office for the meeting.

Miraculously, it was—at first. I could hear them reading books in her room down the hall. I signed into the digital courtroom. The judge went through her procedures and spoke to one divorcing couple after another but not to us. As each minute ticked by, my blood pressure escalated. My palms were sweating. I knew my time away was limited.

Sure enough, LP burst into the office trailed by the neighbor boy. When he tried to take her hand to lead her out, she threw her tiny toddler body toward me, nearly pulling him over, tears falling from her eyes as she called my name. I felt painfully torn in two as I looked between my daughter and the computer screen.

The judge called the other remaining case, which meant our case was next. I panicked. I carried LP into her room, plopped her down, and asked the neighbor boy, who had an iPhone, to pull up something for LP to watch.

"Winnie-the-Pooh?" he asked.

At my nod, he quickly pulled up Disney+ on his phone.

I sprinted back to my computer in time for what ended up being an overview of our divorce petition and acknowledgment that we wanted to move forward. The judge was skimming so fast through the process I doubt she'd have noticed an elephant sitting on my lap, let alone a toddler. And LP's dad had his camera turned off claiming a bad connection. It was a trivial meeting, really.

What *wasn't* trivial was the guilt and self-recrimination I felt over letting LP watch part of the Pooh episode that day. She had gone almost two-and-a-half years without screen time of any kind.

I had wanted to go much longer. I hadn't wanted her to know that these devices that already took up so much of grown ups' attention also contained a world of child-focused programming. I felt like I was right up there with the person in the smoke-filled boardroom who suggested using Joe Camel to market cigarettes to kids. It may sound absurd, yet these were my thoughts.

The way I saw it, in one moment, an era of her life was over, and we had failed at being screen-free.

I was convinced she'd now want to watch Pooh on every phone she saw.

Like most of my worst fears, that did not happen. She never pointed to my phone for Pooh. She never even asked the neighbor boy to watch it again. It was as if the episode never happened. We were no longer perfectly screen-free, but she went right back to not having screen time again.

Still, I submerged myself in vivid feelings of failure.

Looking back, I see that LP may have been screen-free, but I certainly wasn't screen freed.

I wasn't consciously choosing or not choosing screen time based on what was best for everyone in the situation. I was blindly following a rule without regard to *my* needs and the impact my needs had on my daughter. In doing so, I used up far too much of my mental real estate berating myself for an acceptable reaction to my rock-and-a-hard-place situation.

I know I am not alone in beating myself up. I'd wager every single parent has a memory of a time they catastrophized a small choice in parenting, only to look back on it later and realize it wasn't that big of a deal.

My great hope is that we can unshackle ourselves from all-or-nothing paradigms entirely. That we can own and accept our choices—including the ones that a *perfect* parent (eye roll) wouldn't make—and in doing so, find peace. I hope we can set aside the pursuit of perfection and settle in to learn and grow into screen freedom together.

Don't let this book do to you what my rule did to me: Set a standard that is too rigid for your humanity. Instead, let's choose to be intentional about how, why, and when we allow screens into our children's lives.

CHAPTER 5

Why Screen Freedom During Travel?

A FTER MORE THAN 120 SCREEN-FREE TRIPS WITH MY DAUGHTER, I want the magic of screen freed travel to be accessible for all families.

The purpose of writing about screen freed travel comes down to three reasons, and they're all about you:

One, practicing screen freedom during travel makes the at-home boundaries that much easier to uphold.

Many parents have told me that they rely on screen time *more* during travel. They cite factors like long wait and transit times, a desire for their children not to disrupt other travelers, known shows and games bringing familiarity to an unfamiliar environment, and feeling like it's what everyone does after seeing families around them using screens.

If it's harder to avoid screen reliance during travel, then getting good at going without it during travel may make it easier at home. After all, if your kids can go without screens at 30,000 feet in the air or in the backseat on a five-hour road trip, they can definitely do it with a backyard and a house full of toys at home.

Two, travel is a time to focus on being in the moment.

You're spending extra time and effort to be there. Why waste that staring at the apps and shows you have at home? Instead, could you create unforgettable memories with your child by learning about a new place, exploring new experiences, talking with them, and engaging in the moment together?

Screens get in the way of presence. They steal our eye contact and attention from each other and the world around us. While they may numb uncomfortable feelings like boredom, they also dim our sense of curiosity, our zest for adventure, our awareness of the environment, and our connection to our bodily sensations (the feeling of being "in your body"). Screens are not entirely without merit of course. But they are not the path to being connected to life.

Three, travel is for exploration.

Travel is a time not only to try out new places, customs, and foods, but also ideas. Travel offers us freedom and space to investigate different ways of being outside the confines of regular life. In a new environment, our brains are primed for change. What a perfect opportunity to explore your family's relationship to screens and test drive some changes.

CHAPTER 6

Actually Back Up—Why Even Travel With Kids *at All*?

NYONE WHO HAS VACATIONED WITH THEIR CHILDREN AND EXPERIenced an adults-only vacation is acutely aware of the stark differences between the two. One leaves us feeling refreshed and 10 years younger ... and one is traveling with kids.

But remember the magic of travel is also amplified with kiddos.

Plus, did you know that your child can act as a real life Disneyland fast pass?

Dear France, I love you ...

We stood in the line outside the Louvre under the warm French sun. From her stroller, 9-month-old LP looked around with her usual attentiveness. Suddenly a woman touched my arm. I followed her gaze to the man she was pointing to. He was gesturing at my little family.

I stepped forward with trepidation. Were we in trouble? What could we have done wrong? My French was limited to a few polite phrases; I wasn't going to be able to understand or defend myself if he didn't speak English.

As we approached him, his face remained serious, almost stern. We got within speaking distance and he said, in a voice tinged with reproach, "*You do not wait in line.*"

He ushered us in the front door and into a small, open lift. They scanned our tickets and released us to explore the Louvre, while the rest of the line slowly trickled in. I experienced, for the first time in my life, what it's like to get the VIP treatment of a celebrity.

This occurred again and again. All over Paris, we were repeatedly escorted to the front of the line because of our baby. It happened at tourist spots and even when awaiting transportation. Before our outbound flight, they bumped us ahead of all the passengers to pass through customs. And no, it wasn't because LP was a screaming baby they wanted to move along.

Why am I sharing this story? Because you never know how a place will surprise you. Veteran international travelers will tell you that French people don't have the friendliest reputation. When I actually went there, I discovered a totally different reality.

Isn't that what travel is all about? Replacing rumors and bias with real-life truths? Don't we want to raise curious little humans who seek out their own knowledge over secondhand narratives that may not be true?

This is one solid reason to travel with kids, but there are even more.

Everybody's Doing It!

The great news is, when everyone is doing it, we tend to find a lot more accommodations and it becomes normalized.

We all watched *Home Alone*, right? We know that people were flying with kids in the 1990s. But it wasn't nearly as common as it is now. Many factors have changed since then accounting for the increase in family travel, including comparatively lower flight prices, more available flights, ease of booking flights without a travel agent, and for the Millennial generation, an expectation that travel is part of life.

Across nearly all measured travel behaviors, Millennials outpace other generations, even wealthier Baby Boomers, for frequency of travel. "[Millennials] see travel as a right rather than a privilege, and consider their travel experiences to be a part of their identity rather than a check on a bucket list," says Lindsey Roeschke, travel and hospitality analyst. Isn't it incredible that we will likely raise our children to prioritize exploring the world?

A 2018 Resonance Consultancy report called *Future of U.S. Millennial Travel* indicated 44% of Millennial travelers bring their children with them on vacation. Of traveling Millennial families, 62% do it with kids under the age of five (*whew*!), according to insights by D.K. Shifflet & Associates.

So … welcome to the Adventure Club!

The best news of travel becoming more prevalent? When your kid starts crying on a plane or bus or ferry (because at some point, he will), you can take comfort in knowing the folks up front don't know if it's your kid or one of the other half dozen small humans.

Travel Is a Gift With Endless Opportunities for Magic

Travel gives to the whole family and cultivates:

- Happier, more fulfilled parents
- Unforgettable memories
- Broader cultural exposure and appreciation
- Opportunity for worldwide friendships
- Practice socializing in new settings
- Flexibility regarding change
- Curiosity and a sense of adventure
- Confidence

Having a tiny sidekick will change and even improve the way you travel. Traveling with kids can be an extra level (*okay, three levels*) of complicated and exhausting, but contained within the challenges are gifts.

More rest.

Because my daughter, until recently, needed a nap, I've napped too. Before kids, I would wring every minute out of my trips, especially the expensive overseas adventures. Now, I nap or read a book in the middle of the day, regardless of whether I'm in Paris or Portland.

It's nice to step out of the pressured frenzy of gobbling up a new place and make space for rest. And it's not just naps. The pace of your family travel will change, and I think it's an improvement.

There's more sitting in random parks. Meals are slower and often at eateries with locals rather than tourist-touted hot spots or fancy restaurants. Locals approach to coo at the baby and sometimes those moments turn into real conversations and meaningful interactions. Maybe you will see a bit less, but you'll experience the places you visit on a deeper level at a more peaceful pace.

▨ More presence.

Not only am I more observant out of vigilance for safety, I've traveled moving at a toddler, preschooler, and now, kindergartener-pace. As your kids slow you down, you'll have a chance to see more.

But it's more than just moving slowly. Your amazing little person is basically an alien to the planet. She'll point out all the things she sees, scenes your eyes might have passed right over. Children are tourists everywhere they go because all places are new to them.

You'll benefit from their eagle eyes that seem attuned to the good stuff—a message on the sidewalk that turned out to be bits of poetry carved into cement, a children's toy shop in a quiet French town that contains locally carved wooden delights, a tiny, hidden park at the end of a sleepy alley, and a friendly stranger who confides the best kept bakery secret in the neighborhood.

▨ More appreciation.

I don't jetset with the frequency of my pre-mom days, and likely you won't either. So when you get to go, with or without your children, you'll cherish it more. Even though the numbers of traveling families are rising, still relatively few parents will see a lot of the world through their children's eyes. Though travel is work, it's also a privilege. Remembering this makes it easy to find reasons to be grateful every time you board a plane or step on the gas pedal headed toward adventure.

▨ More awe.

Kids give us reason to pause to think about the wonder of human invention that enables you to power across a channel on a ferry, traverse a country in a day by bus or train, and fly over oceans into foreign lands in mere hours. When you explain these feats to your children, you reveal them to yourself too.

Next time you board a plane, I dare you to imagine that you could instead be bumping along in a covered wagon on a death-defying sojourn across rugged terrain. If you're anything other than floored with wonder and gratitude for flying, then you clearly didn't play Oregon Trail enough as a kid. From the invention of the wheel to where we are now, of all the times we could've been born into, we were born into this age. Into this freedom.

Into this relative safety of travel. Into this era in which exploration is a plane ticket or tank of gas away. How incredible!

It Gets Easier With Practice

Another gift of taking more adventures with your kids is that the practice makes each subsequent adventure easier.

Recently, my daughter and I took an impromptu road trip to be with family. The drive is 350 miles and takes about seven hours. On Thursday, we decided to go. We pulled out of the garage by 8 a.m. on Friday morning and we were parked at my brother's townhome by 3 p.m.

(Bear in mind, we've been doing this drive for six years. I am not suggesting you plan and undertake your first road trip with kids within 18 hours. But that's how ours began.)

During the road trip, we alternately talked, listened to an audiobook together, listened to audiobooks separately, stopped to play in some mountainside woods, sat in silence, and sang silly songs. With her little kid scissors, a stack of paper, and a bag of markers, LP made countless pieces of art.

The seven hours flew by and the only pain I experienced was a stiff back as I climbed out of the car and stretched at our destination.

It was not only painless; it was fun.

A roadtrip with a 5-year-old was fun, no screens needed.

That might sound unbelievable. If you'd told me it was possible when she was a baby, I might not have believed it either. At that time, I wasn't shooting for *fun* road trips alone with my daughter; I was happily settling for "uneventful."

But it is possible. LP and I travel often, and the trips are mostly a blast. Other than packing, they require little more effort on my part than our regular life.

The ease isn't because my child is exceptional. In fact, she is bold with a strong personality, an immense drive to have things done her way, and a critical mind that doesn't accept a superficial answer (which she *may* have inherited from me). Travel with her personality type could be rife with conflict and nonstop demands, leading me to seek out a screensitter.

But it's not, because we have tools, a strong mindset, and a lot of practice.

If your first trip with your kid was a bit of a nightmare, take heart! The next will get easier. And the next one after that easier still. The more you travel, the more you'll be able and willing to travel.

CHAPTER 7

Let's Gooooo

W E HAVE SPENT SIX CHAPTERS GETTING HERE, AND THAT'S required courage from every part of you. On some level, you want screen freedom. Maybe it's in the forefront, or maybe it's still marinating in the back of your mind. Show up where you are. If that means you have doubts, fears, or worries at this stage, I've got you. I'll be confident enough for both of us while you're still navigating the way.

The reality is we are far more capable than we realize. So are our children. And we can actively grow this capability too.

Doing hard things enables us to do other hard things. It's why I run Spartan obstacle course races. Sure, they're fun. They're also a training ground for life. Every time I push past the point in the race when I think I can't finish, I become more capable of handling other difficulties or challenges in life. I build my capacity.

We think of pushing ourselves physically as a good training ground for the body. But it's most effective at training our mindset. In races, it's never my body that wants to give up first. It's my mind. My brain receives the inputs from my body (this hurts, this is uncomfortable), and my mind makes a *judgment* about them. That judgment has its finger on the " give up/keep going" toggle switch. The more often it slides toward "give up," the easier that slide becomes. The more we practice doing hard things, as Glennon Doyle says, the more we are willing to face the next challenge.

This is the baseline of resilience.

You? You've got this. You, the person showing up to raise kids every day. You, the person who has lived all the way up to this point, despite the fact that you had the option to give up. You, the person who is choosing conscious parenting knowing it's harder, because you believe in doing what's best for your babies.

You're a damn warrior, and don't let anyone—especially yourself—say you're not equal to the task of traveling screen freed. You and your family are certainly deserving of the gifts on the other side of screen freedom.

In the next chapter, we'll get into the four main reasons people give up before they even try to travel screen freed. If you fall into that category, I've got great news for you.

Once you identify and acknowledge your reasons for giving up or backing off, you have the option to change them. Because they're *your* reasons, so you can choose to un-believe them anytime you want.

Isn't it the best *and the worst* when you find out your mindset is the biggest obstacle (or the key) to something you want?

CHAPTER 8

Have You Said These Things to Yourself?

P EOPLE HAVE AUDIBLY GASPED WHEN I TELL THEM LP HAS NEVER watched anything on a screen in 65 flights and 51 road trips. They gasp as if I said I carried her on my back to summit Everest. When I debuted the concept for my book—that screen freed travel with kids could be enjoyable—many people straight up said to me, "Oh, I could/would never do that."

The reality is that any parent could fly screen-free with their child if they had to. If all their devices died two minutes into the flight, they wouldn't run to the cockpit demanding the pilot turn the plane around. They would figure it out.

But because most people aren't put in the situation where they *have* to figure it out, they let certain beliefs stop them from even trying. Here are the four primary perspectives that get in people's way when they consider traveling screen freed.

1. I need screens.

If you don't think you can be screen freed, it's not entirely your fault. Parents are constantly fed messaging that suggests we aren't quite enough for the task of raising these kids. We must carefully guard our mindset and the words we use to tell the story of our lives to avoid believing this bogus messaging.

Screen Freed is an adaptable approach. Devices are part of our modern lives for utility and entertainment. The fundamental difference lies in how we view our relationship to screen time as it pertains to parenting.

Do you see screens as one tool of many to be used purposefully when the pros outweigh the cons? Or do you see screen time as something you can't function without—something that you need?

Believing we need something that is not life or death is the definition of dependence. When we let ourselves become dependent on something, we are less prone to come up with alternative solutions, consider all the pros and cons, and make informed decisions. What's most concerning is that dependence is a precursor to addiction.

The dependent mindset is revealed when parents make statements like "I couldn't possibly do it without screens," "We can't get through a day without the iPad; I need it," or "What are you nuts? My family could never travel screen-free."

Those who believe screens are a tool, rather than a lifeline, are able to consciously choose when and why to use that tool. They're willing to be a bit more scientific about usage and experiment by stepping away from screens to see what happens.

They make statements like, "We are choosing to have a family movie night," "I'd like to be fully present for this meeting, and being interrupted by my child will prevent that. I'm choosing to let him have screen time for the duration," and "It will be faster to learn how to make a bird feeder from this YouTub video. Let's watch it together." They don't diminish their abilities by saying that they need screens to parent. They know they always have a choice in regard to screen time. When they choose it, they own the choice.

The nuance really matters. The language of choice is empowering. It puts us in the driver's seat of our behavior versus suggesting we are inadequate to the task of parenting and we need screens to make up the difference. This frees us from a dependent relationship with screens.

A parent who believes they need screens won't consider traveling with little or no screen time. There are so many more options available to parents who know they don't need screens (but may sometimes choose them), because they are free to consider what they are capable of.

2. I'm the only one.

Wanting to belong is a normal human desire. Humans are tribal and social animals who have survived by aligning ourselves with a community. Within the community, we bond over like-minded values and similar experiences in order to form peer groups. It can feel scary to do things differently than our peers.

When making counter-cultural choices, you may worry about being ostracized or making others feel uncomfortable.

This worry makes sense, but you shouldn't let it dictate your behavior. Any group that would ostracize you for making safe parenting choices isn't a healthy group. And we can't *make* anyone else feel uncomfortable. Our choices may highlight for others what they want to but are unwilling to do. That can feel uncomfy for them. But that's their journey. Your journey is to choose what's best for yourself and your family.

History has shown us that majority approval doesn't make something right. There are more people parenting in reactive mode than parenting consciously. Though we all sometimes dip into survival mode, you're reading this book because you want to parent consciously and work toward making the healthiest, most beneficial choices for your family.

I've spent my life questioning the norms and trends of our society, and I have a ton of practice choosing counter-cultural beliefs and behaviors.

It's fine if you've spent more of your life fitting in or following the trends. But now that you have children, it's your responsibility to question if the masses are right about screens. To be screen freed, I invite you to explore your inner rebel. This means thinking critically about your views and motivations.

Do you feel like everyone else gives devices to their kids? Do you think the collective leaning toward younger and younger screen usage is okay if the majority of people are doing it? Do you feel justified with your screen choices because of what you see other parents doing?

Or … do you want to make more parenting choices based on your own internal guidance system?

You *can* find your own way. You can buck the norm. And you might find, as I have, that other people admire and appreciate your uncommon choices—even if they don't agree with them.

Furthermore, when you choose a different path from the majority, you will find a home with what I call the willingly weird minority. You'll connect with other counter-cultural folks, and your perspective and community become more beautiful for their diversity.

You'll discover how to be a leader, not a follower and in doing so, take back your freedom.

3. I want to give myself a break and make parenting easy.

Ever get the sense we're trying to hack our way to a parenting experience that isn't invasive, confronting, or exhausting? The reality is that parenting is all those things and more. Parenting is the hardest thing I've ever done, and next-level challenges are kind of my MO. Raising my daughter trumps every hard thing I've done combined.

So what's wrong with trying to make this parenting gig a bit easier?

Nothing!

We should learn from one another, share tips and tools, enroll help, and more. Yes to all of this! It is a good idea to do things that make parenting easier as long as the benefits outweigh the costs.

But parenting is never going to be *easy*.

We could have all the support in the world, and as long as we are parents, there will be challenges. It's in the job description. The landscape of our kids' development and needs changes so fast it can feel like we're running across the ground in an earthquake. Some days, it's all we can do to stay upright.

When we don't call parenting what it is—hard—we are in danger of defaulting to screens.

Parents who want to make parenting easy are more likely to make choices that get them what they want in the moment but don't necessarily contribute to their long-term goals or values. Enter: the iPad easy button.

You're reading this book because you have chosen to be a conscious parent. So you've probably already realized:

Choosing conscious parenting *is* choosing the harder path.

Once you can accept and even embrace that, you're free to parent based on your values, not on an endless pursuit of easy.

4. Kids are on screens. It's just the way the world is now.

I'm not going to spend a lot of time on this one. I am writing this book and you're reading it, because we already agree that reducing screen time is a good aim.

But some of us have sort of hazy reasons for wanting to reduce screen time. We know too much screen time isn't great, but we don't really understand what is lost when screens are on.

A fuzzy or soft "why" isn't going to get you through the tougher travel moments.

A powerful "why" can cut through your own (and others') second-guessing and thoughts of giving up. Chapter 19 details some (but certainly not all) of the downsides of screen time for young kids. My hope is that it will fuel your screen freedom resolution. But first, I'll share some mindset tools that will enable you to get the most out of Chapter 19, the rest of the book, and your screen freed travel experience.

CHAPTER 9

Mindset Tools

MINDSET HAS BECOME A BUZZWORD, BUT THE DIFFERENCE BETWEEN *talking* about it and *applying* it often means the difference between succeeding or not.

But first, a disclaimer:

Parenting books are naturally confronting. We pick them up because we want help with some aspect of parenting. But along the way, the author tells us how they think we could or should be doing things differently. Suddenly, we feel guilt, shame, or regret, despite the fact that we chose the book, because we *wanted* to do things differently.

I remember reading *The Importance of Being Little* by Erika Christakis (a great read for parents of preschoolers) and feeling so sad as I recounted all the times my expectations for my 4-year-old daughter's behavior were far beyond her development.

I wish I had known better sooner.

It's normal to feel this way.

While regret or guilt *can* motivate us to do things differently, they aren't effective as the primary inspiration for action. Those emotions too easily lead to defensiveness. When we feel the need to defend ourselves, we reduce our capacity for learning. Our minds shut down to new information. Simple facts can start to feel like an attack. To reduce our discomfort, we may go offense by looking for someone to attack or make the "bad guy."

If the information I share brings up uncomfy feelings, remember, I am on your side. Everything I say is because I am fiercely invested in you and your family having it *all* as travelers. Having it all means closer relationships, calm, a deeper connection, a sense of curiosity, presence, and epic adventures.

Just like you, I feel the invisible weight of the scrutiny we parents are under. I've dealt with the same level of judgment—from myself and others—that you face.

The following chapter contains some of the mindset tools I use to navigate sensitive topics related to my parenting. Not only will these tools help on your journey toward screen freedom, they're also useful across life.

Mindset Tool #1: Mapping Your Beliefs

Later, I'll give an overview of some of the potential negative outcomes of screen time. That's not the primary purpose of *Look Up!*, but it will come up naturally in the course of discussing strategies for reducing screen usage during travel.

Tool #1: Begin a practice of checking in with yourself to *notice and name* how you feel.

This book is a great testing ground because you can identify how you feel when you read about the potential negative outcomes of screen time.

As parents, we've adapted to be able to set aside "our stuff" to meet the demands of whatever situation needs us. This is a great skill to have when there's a crisis or emergency or when the little humans are heated, and we need to be calm to bring the household thermostat to a normal temp.

However, continuously overlooking or subduing how we feel and not exploring why we feel that way doesn't support our long-term growth.

Noticing and naming our emotions is a powerful way to listen to ourselves and discover the beliefs we have about a situation, the person in front of us, our identity as parents, or even our lives. These beliefs drive our emotions. Think of a strong emotion as a little flag planted in a spot where a belief lives. By checking in and identifying the emotion, you can trace it back to the belief that is under it.

Before we get into why belief identification matters so much, it's important to address something about feelings.

Emotions can be tricky! The first one we feel often belongs to the category of feelings we were taught are acceptable. It takes presence and practice to sift through the surface-level emotions to what's going on beneath.

Growing up, I got the message that being vulnerable was not safe. So when I feel emotions that feel vulnerable to me, such as fear, confusion, or powerlessness, I express them as fury.

For example, this can happen when I don't know how to handle a change in my daughter's behavior. When I reach for a healthy response in my parenting toolkit and come up empty-handed, I feel powerless. But powerlessness feels vulnerable. So I might express it as anger, because I was taught that being mad was acceptable. Now, when I feel anger, I know to dig around underneath for the vulnerable feeling it is shielding.

Generation, culture, gender, and the family we grew up in can all influence which emotions we feel free to express and which ones we avoid or submerge. Typically, women receive messaging their anger is not acceptable but sadness is. Conversely, many men are taught to express most of their emotions as anger, even when they actually feel fear or grief.

When you notice the emotion that rises up first, see if you can peel it back to something else. It takes practice to get to the root emotion, but you can do it.

One simple question to continue asking yourself once you've felt the initial emotion is, "What's under there?"

Here are some feelings that might come up during your screen freed journey: Fear, grief, shame, loneliness, embarrassment, or unworthiness.

Building our capacity to notice and identify these deeper, painful emotions also enables us to identify and feel the whole spectrum of emotions including the ones that feel good like joy, strength, peace, fulfillment, gratitude, groundedness, and bravery.

Getting back to the importance of identifying our beliefs via our feelings, take this example:

Molly notices that as she's traveling without screens for the first time, her son is more fussy. She sees people giving her son side looks, and she feels angry. As she investigates the emotion, she discovers that she's actually embarrassed. She spent a lot of her childhood silently embarrassed, because she grew up in a loud family of five kids who were side-eyed everywhere they went. She realizes that the embarrassment is a sign of a belief she has that by being disruptive, *she* is humiliating and unlovable.

As she uncovers the belief, she's able to see that sideways looks and a little fussiness is what is happening, but it's her belief that is telling her she's unlovable and humiliating. When she identifies this and works to overturn that belief, she's able to be more present with the actual circumstances. Molly realizes she can, in fact, weather the situation, because she no longer has to deal with the belief tearing her down on top of the reality of a fussy kiddo and judgemental strangers.

Our beliefs are in the driver's seat of our actions. Repeated actions become our habits. The accumulation of our habits equals the results we have in our lives.

If we aren't aware of what beliefs are driving us, we will not be able to enact meaningful change that gets us what we want.

Let's say we want to change a result or do something new—such as travel screen freed. We can try to do it by only changing our actions. But that means we have to resist the way our beliefs want us to behave. This is far more difficult and less successful than if we simply changed at the belief level. If you adopt the belief that yours is a limited screen family, it's far easier to behave as such.

In the course of exploring your beliefs, you may uncover many that you don't want to change. These are helpful to discover too!

Throughout this book, work to notice how you feel and what beliefs are fueling those feelings. Are those beliefs you actually agree with? Or were they handed to you in childhood or by society? Are your beliefs supporting you to grow and have what you want in life? Or are they holding you back, limiting your openness, or causing you to doubt yourself?

This mindset tool is a lifelong practice. Everybody has beliefs that limit them and beliefs that give them beautiful results. The practice of awakening to your beliefs is one that will serve you at every age and stage of life. And it will empower you to make life changes you never before thought possible.

Check In:

This is a hefty mindset tool. Don't feel compelled to start unpacking every belief you have and assessing them. Start small with one emotion you had recently. When you trace it back to the belief behind it, what is it? Where did the belief come from? Do you agree with it? Is it getting you what you want? If you choose to release it, what belief could replace it that supports your best life?

Mindset Tool #2: Two Things Are True

We've all met or seen parents online who only talk about how great parenting is. They'll wax on and on about the heartwarming bliss of being a parent. But they seem to not experience—or at least not acknowledge—the hard or messy parts. In the face of someone spouting only parental bliss, it's an act of bravery to admit that it's damn hard.

Just as the idyllic portrayal of parenthood is only part of the story, so is the other side that finds its way into TV shows, movies, and influencer posts: Parenthood as a never-ending hellscape. I love a hilarious meme or a heartfelt reel depicting a parenting struggle, but exposure to too many of these can cause me to start viewing mama-life through a negative filter. Yes, it can be hard, uncomfortable, and overwhelming, but raising kids isn't *all* bad either.

To have honest conversations about the experience of parenthood, we need more expansive and inclusive stories. Our brains don't like this so much. They love to organize things into tidy boxes. But rarely is reality simple or tidy. When we try to force our experiences into a single description or perspective, we can usually only do it by silencing part of our truth. This can leave us feeling unseen and unheard.

Tool #2: *Two things are true.*

I was days into being a mama when I realized I could only describe the complex experience of parenthood by using the axiom *two things are true.*

This statement allows us to acknowledge all of our feelings and responses to a situation, not just the ones that match how we think we "should" feel. It makes room for our entire selves.

In life and especially in parenthood, it often seems like we feel two contradictory things at once. We could be wiping up a blowout with feelings of disgust while also marveling that we made a tiny human capable of such enormous onesie destruction. We can gaze down in awe at our cherubic child as she sleeps and also feel terribly alone. We can acknowledge the hardships and the immense rewards of parenting in a way that gives color and depth where a single perspective is only black and white.

In the case of traveling with my girl, I frequently need two contradictory truths to describe how I felt about the whole experience or about a certain moment:

"Two things are true: Traveling with my daughter is exhausting AND joyous."

"Two things are true: I know I want to travel screen freed AND I want the kind of break screen time might buy me."

"Two things are true: This trip is friggin' hard! I wish it was easier, AND I am still glad I chose it."

"Two things are true: I want to be on this trip AND I don't want to be in this difficult moment."

"Two things are true: I'm grateful to be able to travel with my kid AND I wish I could have some alone time."

Making room for that mental juggling act is a critical skill to develop. We live in a world that demands that we pick a side. We are supposed to slap a title on ourselves, stake our identity on it, and then only say we're perfectly happy with that choice. It's exhausting.

We instinctively know that parenting requires far more flexibility and adaptability. We don't have to accept one-sided viewpoints. Instead, we can create room for the expansive spectrum of parenting and living. We can describe a reality in which two (or more!) opposing things are true at the same time. We can dance in the nuance.

Check In:

What are some recent conversations or experiences that you felt pressured to describe too simply? Can you now expand your view of them with a *two things are true* statement?

Next time you travel with your child, especially in moments of conflict or difficulty, can you practice finding a *two things are true* statement? Consider sharing it with your child, no matter their age. They're never too young to start expressing a more holistic experience.

Mindset Tool #3: A 3-part Framework for Radical Acceptance

All my life, I've had a troubled relationship with acceptance. I used to think of acceptance as giving up or just letting life happen. I would practically roll my eyes out of my head when I heard the phrase "it is what it is."

I much preferred to think of myself as someone who would pursue the best outcome relentlessly and not settle for anything less.

Then I became a parent. Suddenly my outcomes weren't about business and monetary success, earning the A, or physical goals that I could "crush." They weren't quantifiable, and they certainly weren't entirely up to me. My life was inextricably wound up with the life of a brand-new human. There is nothing like an infant to teach you the importance of accepting what is, am I right? But when I reached for the feeling of acceptance, I found it wasn't there. Apparently, it doesn't magically appear along with the baby, which is obviously a rude trick of nature.

Acceptance is easy to practice when things are going our way. But when our loved ones, or our own actions, fail to meet our standards or preferences, acceptance is a skill we have to develop. I learned that acceptance is actually an active process and on the other side of it lives self-knowledge, grace, and growth.

These are the steps I take to practice acceptance:

1. Awareness

Awareness is the result of tuning in and noticing how we feel. Note: If this looks familiar, it is! This is something you have already read about (and maybe even started to practice) in Mindset Tool #1. In a particularly difficult moment of parenting, I don't always know how I feel or understand why I act a certain way. I'm caught up in navigating the situation in front of me.

Later, I need quiet time to reflect on the situation, to sift through my expectations for myself and others, and to feel all my feelings, especially the feelings I squashed in order to handle the moment. I've been surprised to realize a surface emotion like irritation can so effectively cover up a deeper one like grief, embarrassment, shame, or a fear of failure. When we dig deep to discover our core feelings, we can see how they drive our choices and behavior.

Awareness of our own limiting beliefs and deep emotions can help us feel empathy for other people too. We start to see how their big surface emotion might be shielding a really uncomfortable vulnerable one underneath.

In Chapter 10, I share how it took a completely stressful (and sweaty, so sweaty) flight with LP for me to become aware of how one of my beliefs about myself as a parent was creating a shame cycle.

2. Sharing

Awareness starts inside of us, but it's most beneficial to share it. This may look like journaling or saying it out loud to yourself or another person. My sister says I'm an external processor; I always feel better when I call my mom or best friend and tell them what I discovered.

In her book *Daring Greatly*, Brene Brown tells us that shame festers in the dark. Speaking a thing out loud to a safe person, even if the story doesn't portray us at our best, is the fastest and most effective way to shine light on what happened. A burden in the light heals faster than one in the darkness of our sometimes unkind internal dialogue.

Especially when I wish I hadn't handled a situation a certain way, like yelling at my daughter, snapping at a colleague, or rage-eating half a pan of brownies, I find it helpful to share with someone who loves me uncon- ditionally. Such a conversation can become a pathway to healing when the person we tell receives our story with empathy or says "me too" or helps us see the latent humor. If we are recounting the way another person trespassed against us, simply hearing another person say, "That must have felt bad," or "That sounds hard," can be a salve.

Not every person is a safe place to share your deepest realizations, cringiest moments, or biggest struggles with loved ones. Just because someone is in our family or has known us a long time, doesn't mean they have capacity to hold space for our vulnerable moments. I suggest choosing people who are doing work on themselves too. Steer clear of those who cling to toxic views or who will encourage you to justify your actions or to blame others and not take responsibility for your part. Sarcasm and perfectionism are also not traits of someone safe to share with.

For example, let's say you've vocalized that you want to travel screen-free but you recently let your son watch *Bluey* on a train trip. Choose the person with the emotional intelligence to say, "I know traveling without screens is really important to you. I'm glad you shared this with me, because I get a chance to tell you that you're still a great parent! Your son is so lucky to have you. Would you like me to keep listening or would you like to brainstorm solutions to stay off screens for future trips?"

3. Acceptance

The truth is that life will not always go the way we prefer. When it doesn't, we may experience big and difficult feelings. In response to those feelings, we will sometimes act in ways we wish we hadn't. (Congrats, you're not perfect—that would be boring!) Once this has happened, we can't undo it. We can only work to accept that it happened, and find out why in order to do better next time.

Acceptance and justification are *not* the same.

To accept that it happened is not the same as justifying what we did. As we practice all the steps of acceptance and are honest with ourselves, we can see that we have a choice in every single interaction. This responsibility is a sort of freedom, because it means we are not at the whim of the world.

Acceptance, not justification, gives us the capacity for heartfelt apologies when needed, for learning from our past choices, for being open to feedback, for practicing new ways of being, and for making different choices in the future.

Our aim is to replace shame with acceptance, because as we talked about earlier, shame is a shoddy long-term motivator. Sometimes the thing we feel ashamed about is outside of our control. Shame then becomes a prison we're locked inside because we think we need to change the circumstance instead of changing how we view the circumstance.

Acceptance is like a broom. It cleans up messes, especially the ones we made for ourselves. It sweeps in the dark corners to get the shame cobwebs. It clears away the story to reveal what simply is *without* judgment. Through acceptance, we process our experiences—good, bad, and everything in between.

The best news is we can find acceptance for things that happened five minutes ago or thirty years ago.

Sometimes this process is simple. It's a great tool for getting through the daily frustrations, unmet expectations, and conflicts. Other times, especially for events that happened to us rather than things we've done, we may need the help of a professional. Eye Movement Desensitization and Reprocessing (EMDR) is an extensively researched, effective therapeutic technique proven to help PTSD, trauma, phobias, anxiety, and more. Please don't hesitate to seek the support you need.

Check In:

Can you think of any experiences you haven't fully accepted? Are there things you've done that you still feel shame about? Or things that were done to you that still feel a big reaction toward? What happens after you go through the steps of acceptance regarding those experiences? Do you feel a new lightness, like you had been carrying around a weight that you didn't even know was there?

CHAPTER 10

How Beliefs Can Be Your Fastpass to Grand Adventure ... or Not

L ET'S LEARN HOW TO CHOOSE BELIEFS AND EXPECTATIONS THAT MAKE travel easier and more fun—even with kids and *without* devices.

Traveling screen freed is about much more than what toys you pack for a long flight or what snacks will least destroy your backseat on a road trip (the answer is none of them, your backseat is doomed).

All parenting, and especially the screen freed variety, is a mind game. The more healthy, adaptable, and strong our beliefs as parents, the better the whole experience can be for us and our children. A healthy mindset is like a muscle in our body; unused, it will weaken. Just like a muscle, we can strengthen it with different mental exercises that ensure our views are balanced and agile enough to get us through difficult situations.

But First, a Story

It was happening. Oh yes, it was happening, and I couldn't stop it.

LP was going to lose it.

I was quickly losing it myself.

I had told her to do something.

She protested, "But Mama!"

I told her to calm down, but I should have been telling myself. I gritted out commands for silence through clenched teeth—a surefire way to ignite a 3-year-old into defiance. That's exactly what it did.

Her tiny fists balled up. Her blue eyes opened wide, compelling me to understand what she needed. The toddler explosion was coming. Instead of calming myself for the careful work of a bomb-defuser, I had lit the fuse.

"Stop kicking the seat in front of you, and tell me what you need in a calm voice," I demanded in what could hardly be construed as *my* calm voice.

My heart was racing. My fingers dug into my thighs. My face was already red with an embarrassed blush.

I was cataloging who around me would be quickest to judge us—the old lady with the perma-pursed lip lines? The "just gonna check a final email while we taxi despite being told to put away my laptop" man in the suit? The poor unfortunate soul who'd chosen the aisle seat in our row?

"MAMAAAAAAAA!"

That day, the situation escalated because of how I responded. I don't even remember what the original issue was; I just recall her screaming at the top of her lungs on the airplane. I remember the mortification I felt. A small part of my brain empathized with how frustrated and helpless she must have felt to resort to such an outburst. But mostly, I was mad.

So how did this happen?

When the conflict arose, it was fairly minor. But I wasn't present to it. Instead, I was focused on not disturbing the passengers around me. I made the moment about them and their comfort.

I prioritized silencing a small person with an undeveloped brain. I showed her that I was more interested in controlling her behavior than resolving the conflict.

Personally, I do not advocate for feral parenting or letting kids do whatever they want despite how it affects others. I believe it's part of my duty as a parent to teach LP that she shares the public world and that her actions affect other people.

However that day, I was way more concerned about my role as a fellow passenger than my role as a parent. I didn't employ all my parenting and emotional regulation skills and lean into my relationship with LP to help the situation; instead, I tried to be a human mute button. The approach failed, and when I regulated my emotions, I apologized to LP.

In the rest of this chapter, we'll get into how our beliefs get in our way like mine did that day, and how you can work to keep the same thing from happening to you.

Not My Monkeys, Not My Circus

In the mindset chapter, we discussed how our beliefs are the source of our emotions. This is critical information because it turns out our feelings influence our children too. I know, *sigh*.

Children can feel our stress and worry. Mirror neurons are partly responsible for the bonded connection between children and caregivers. These neurons enable babies and children to quickly perceive changes in our mood or disposition. This is because on a biological level, such changes may indicate our ability or desire to protect them. This is a very primitive function. Primitive functions unconsciously trigger quick and strong responses, because they are meant to keep us alive at all costs.

When we parents feel big emotions like fear, anger, or anxiety, our children are tuned in and can feel it too. If little ones are also feeling similar emotions, the added input from our feelings can overwhelm them. The good news is that our calm, contentment, and love can also influence them. *Whew!*

That's why much of this book is about working through our feelings and experiences as parents. Because faking it doesn't work—our kids know what's really up. Our real feelings can steer the ship for our whole family (no pressure but like ... pressure).

Now let's talk about who you do not have that kind of influence over: fellow travelers who aren't in your family.

You are not bonded to them. Their mirror neurons are not attuned to yours. You cannot soothe them by being calm yourself.

Have you heard the saying, "not my monkeys, not my circus" as a way to distinguish what is not our responsibility?

Well, if they're not in your family, they're not your monkeys.

Their circus is not yours either.

So if they're not in your circus, they don't need to be your focus. You read about me learning this the hard way in the preceding story. Don't be like me. Instead, make your own circus your focus (once I became a mother, I could really appreciate the comic title *Family Circus*). You can't manage the hoops, juggling, animals, and tightrope walkers if you're running out of the tent to check on other circuses.

The "not my circus" mindset applies to the strangers around you as well as anyone who might be trying to reach you via phone or email. What boundaries can you put in place so that you're able to be fully focused on your family during your trip? If stepping away from work isn't possible the entire time, can you contain work to certain hours and set up support for your kids during those times? Doing both at once will not only strain your nervous system, it will ensure you're giving neither role your best.

What can you delegate? Can you set expectations ahead of time for other people who rely on you? I find that honoring the boundaries set by my colleagues when *they're* out of office is the most surefire way to get the same from them when I'm gone.

Sometimes there isn't actually interference from others, but we assume there will be and react to that with anxiety. What would it be like if you gave yourself permission to be present right where you are with the only people you can influence in that moment—your family?

During travel, do your best to clear space to be present to your precious circus. The space that needs to be cleared isn't only in your external life. It's internal too. It's about figuring out what travel-related beliefs are taking up space in your mind (and showing up in your feelings and behaviors) that are not supporting your best experience. That's where I found myself in the story in the next section.

The great news is that when you have all your energy with you in the present moment, you realize that the circus is actually quite entertaining and fun, especially when the snacks are plentiful. Yippee, break out the popcorn!

Check In:

What systems do you need to set up before traveling to give yourself space to be focused on only your circus? Does your work culture support taking time away, and if not, is that something you can influence? Is the boundary you need to set with others or within?

When the Past Barges into the Present

Before I was a parent, I was on a cross-country flight during which a toddler had screamed on and off for two hours while his parents chatted and watched things on their phones. I have no idea if the child had neurological or emotional challenges, but it was a brutal flight experience. At first, I tried to give his parents the benefit of the doubt. But it looked, to me, like the parents were going about their business while their child screamed in the seat between them, pausing his caterwauling only briefly to eat or drink. I walked off that flight with a massive headache and a vow that I would never be like *those parents.*

It wasn't the crying child I had an issue with (mostly); it was his parents' lack of visible effort to calm or help him that drove me nuts. It wasn't until my first flight with LP that I realized how much that experience shaped my beliefs about traveling with a baby.

We left at 5 in the morning for Portland, just the two of us. LP was 7 months old. From the trunk, I unloaded enough luggage to look like we were embarking on an around-the-world trip. On my back was the baby bag, stuffed full. My purse crisscrossed my chest. LP rode in her infant seat atop her big wheeled cruiser stroller. I had a pack 'n play balanced precariously on the stroller storage under her seat. With giant tires meant to absorb any bump or pebble that might cause its rider a jolt, maneuverability was *not* the stroller's main selling point. It was unwieldy and nearly impossible to steer with one arm. While pushing her stroller, I drug a massive suitcase by hooking my right arm through its handle.

I looked like a bag lady as I tripped along, periodically slamming the suitcase into my heel. We boarded a bus to the terminal thanks to extensive help from the bus driver. With sheepish gratitude, I offloaded the enormous suitcase and pack 'n play to the desk agent at check-in. LP rewarded my newfound luggage-freedom with a super wet diaper that soaked through her leggings and required an outfit change.

By the time we boarded the plane, I was already sweaty, disgruntled, and exhausted. I chose a seat for us at the back of the plane where it's loudest. This is one of my pro tips. If you're worried about your child's noise, it'll be muffled in the back of the plane because it's very loud. The plane noise is kind of womb-like and can soothe little ones to sleep. Plus, you're near the bathrooms. Best of all, it places you in close proximity to flight attendants, which can really come in handy if you're traveling without a co-parent.

As we began to taxi down the runway, I put my plan into action: I would nurse LP during takeoff to help relieve any pressure-related ear pain for her. With any luck, she'd fall asleep and nap the entire flight. Jackpot, a parent with a plan.

Has any veteran parent ever told you that a parenting plan is like a challenge to the gods? If not, sorry you had to learn the hard way like me.

She began nursing, and the plane slowed to a stop. *Weird*, I thought, and hoped we were just lining up to take off. Ten minutes later, we were still stopped. Twenty minutes later, we were still stopped. My baby was happily sucking down the last vestiges of my brilliant plan, and there was no way I was taking the boob away from her. That's basically an act of terrorism in babyland. She finished nursing a bit later, and we still hadn't taken off. Great. I started to nervous-sweat, thinking she was going to flip out during take off.

She didn't, but that didn't stop me from stressing. Despite us traveling during her normal nap time (a pro travel tip that *usually* works), she was active nearly the whole flight. One minute she was looking out the window, enraptured by passing clouds. The next minute she was delightedly swinging her arms around until she clubbed me so hard in the face with a Cabbage Patch doll (my own Cabbage Patch from childhood, *rude!*) that I got a fat lip. She waved at every passenger headed for the bathroom, leading a flight attendant to joke that they should offer her a job.

The whole time I was working on making such big, obvious efforts to calm and contain her that two-thirds of the way through, a flight attendant came by to ask me if I wanted a drink. I mumbled a resentful no (like I was going to add a cup full of liquid to this helicopter arm situation!) and she said, "Oh honey, it's on the house." If that's any indicator, I clearly didn't look like I was having fun.

The thing is ... LP wasn't doing anything excessively disruptive or being very loud. I was jumping all over the situation if it even seemed like she might veer toward less than ideal plane behavior. I wasn't responding to actual reality. Instead, I was reacting to my previous flight experience of the screaming kid and his seemingly unconcerned parents.

That first flight culminated in my baby girl falling asleep on my chest for the last 20 minutes. In the peace and stillness, I reflected on what belief and feelings had driven my frenzied over-parenting. I realized I was afraid of failing to look like a "good parent." I was terrified a stranger on the plane would remember me as a *laissez faire* mama, like I remembered those parents.

I made it harder than it needed to be. LP was delighted to be there. I wish I could've said the same. I brought my mental baggage with me, and it turns out it was heavier and more cumbersome than all the luggage combined.

I had to sort through the story I was telling myself about "good parent-ing." I had to forgive and forget those strangers who ignored their son's screaming. Once I did so, I could find the path to teaching my daughter about manners and societal expectations that wasn't based on my reaction to a past event—or on keeping adults comfy or unfounded developmental expectations (which we'll discuss next!).

Check In:

Have you ever felt frustrated or annoyed with other people's children on flights? Where can you give those past situations some grace? Can you concede, *"They were probably doing the best they could with what they had."*

Then, when you're on a flight, will you have a greater capacity to grant yourself that grace? *"I am doing the best I can with what I have. And so is my child. Whether or not others see that (or agree with it) is none of my business."*

Hot Take: Who's the Adult Here?

This section is one of my favorite, sassy ways to dispel the people-pleasing behaviors that keep us from bringing our best selves to parenting.

When I began traveling regularly about 18 years ago I sat through my fair share of squawking infant flights with only my skull candy headphones to compete with the noise. Admittedly, I became one of the people who inwardly sighed when I saw a baby come on board (at least I didnt outwardly groan or sigh like some passengers when I've boarded with LP).

But even as a childless 20-something, when I read an article about parents of an infant passing out little baggies with earplugs and treats to passengers for having to share the plane with their baby, I was flabbergasted. And not in an "oh how creative, let's pin that idea" way. I was appalled that parents of an infant thought they needed to shield a plane full of *adults* from the potential crying of a brand-new human who has no way to conceive why its ears hurt and its environment is unfamiliar. Where did those poor parents get the message that their baby was such a burden to society? And…

Who's the adult here really?

This effort to protect adults from the existence of children is rather strange, considering every single one of us was a child at one point. Adults, who have had decades to practice emotional regulation, patience, and empathy… they are the ones we need to coddle? It's odd to prioritize the most capable creature instead of the least capable.

Travel is scary or confusing to some adults. It is even more so to small, new humans who don't understand all the environmental changes. Children aren't trying to be disturbing; they're just being new humans.

You will not find any recommendations in these pages about how to build a goodie bag for adults who share planes with babies and toddlers. Mostly because I find that ridiculous, and also because of three words: noise canceling headphones.

Noise canceling headphones are inexpensive now. Earplugs only cost pennies. Even regular headphones playing white noise or music can drown out most surrounding sounds.

Can you see that other adults' expectations really aren't the problem here? It's our expectations as parents. Your focus isn't on your son or daughter if you believe either of these things:

- It's your job to keep adults around you comfortable and happy
- Your baby/toddler/child should not make loud noises in public

If either of these beliefs are driving your actions, you will fail to bring your best parenting self to the table. Or … you will give your child a screen to keep them quiet.

Wanting children to act like silent mini-adults leads a lot of parents to turn to screen-time. Screens are designed to ensnare our attention, and they're particularly good at grabbing hold of children's brains. That's why we see so many kids in transit (or in restaurants) silently staring like zombies at tablets. If your primary outcome is "peace" for the sake of other passengers, screens seem like the viable option. (Until you take the screen away or the battery dies, and your kid has a full-blown meltdown.)

If you want screen freedom, you have to care more about what's best for your child than what's best for the public. You'll have to open yourself up to the possibility that your child may be more vocal or disruptive.

I know that if it was the simple question of who you choose—other people or your kids—you'll always choose your children. There's no contest.

But it's *not* that simple; there are all kinds of really strong beliefs working inside of you trying to get your behavior to align with them. That's why we are doing all of this work together—because until you uncover and examine them, they run your life. Some of those beliefs are why you're so successful today. Others are worth replacing.

I know this isn't an easy path to choose. Some of us, myself included, were wired at a young age to do everything in our power to not displease, bother, annoy, disrupt, or (insert your version of this) others.

If you can relate, here's a new set of beliefs to try on:

- *In order to prioritize protecting my child from screens over keeping everyone around me comfortable, I embrace the belief that adults are responsible for their reactions to children.*
- *I believe that I am responsible for being an attentive parent.*

The great news is that the latter, focusing on your role as caregiver, will usually help your child regulate his emotions better and return to calm. In removing your focus from the other adults in the situation, you have more capacity to be present to your kiddo's needs and to teach him healthy, analog ways to cope with the boredom or discomfort of travel. You're more likely to get the result you want—a calm, happy traveling child who isn't disrupting others. Plus, you'll strengthen your bond along the way.

Check In:

Explore your feelings regarding children on public transit. Do you feel like your family belongs there as much as everyone else? Why or why not? Can you make some room for two things to be true? Your child might make noise or be disruptive, and they are still a good kid and you are still a good parent.

Is the Problem Our Expectations?

Expectations are predictions we make based on our beliefs.

But what if our beliefs about what our children are capable of are … wrong?

So how can we discover what *is* age-appropriate behavior? When we can answer that question, we begin to understand what is at work in a child's mind, body, and nervous system that is driving her behavior. We need a plan for determining what are fair expectations for our children developmentally.

Gauging age appropriate behavior was a surprising struggle for me. By the time my daughter was 3, I was 36. I hadn't been a toddler for three decades, so first-hand knowledge of toddlerhood was out. I couldn't recall how my much-younger siblings had behaved as toddlers and preschoolers either. Over time our memories grow fuzzy. Like *Pollyanna*, our brains tend to downplay the hardships and challenges and glorify the good times.

We often get cues from society. We observe kids around us and notate what we hope our children won't do or what we would like them to do. We watch our friends and family as they parent, we watch strangers parent in real life and online, and we receive plenty of (unsolicited) advice from people around us. These observations can powerfully affect our expectations of children's behavior.

Unfortunately, society isn't a great source. The friends and family who are giving us advice have often fallen victim to that Pollyanna trick of memory. Strangers are a blind grabbag—we can't see all the factors influencing their parenting choices or their children's behavior. We have to be careful about putting too much stock in social media too. Watching a reel or TikTok is like seeing one scene from a full-length movie and thinking we understand the whole film. We all know social media comparisons can wreak havoc on our self-concept and self-esteem.

I had another source for my expectations for LP: me. (It's cringe-worthy to share, but I promised myself I'd tell the truth in this book.) When my daughter was about 3, I realized that I'd begun expecting her to do things the way *I* would do them. I know—ridiculous.

Once she began talking and walking around like a mini adult and engaging in some of the behaviors of a conscientious citizen (taking off her shoes and hanging up her coat when we got home, remembering to say please, showing some planning skills), I majorly upleveled my expectations for *all* of her behavior. I thought, unconsciously, that if she had the prefrontal cortex abilities in one area of her life, they must apply to her whole life. The source of these unrealistic expectations was so subtle it took me a while to notice.

How unfair for my daughter.

Luckily, I started to notice that my expectations were way off-base compared to her abilities. I considered that maybe I was the one with the problem. So I sought out expertise from those who had a scientific, evidence-based knowledge of appropriate behavior for kids: parenting book authors.

This brings us to another input: expert advice based on actual child development. I'm wary of some parenting books (or parenting influencers on Instagram), because every five minutes someone has a new approach to "solve parenting."

However, there *are* experts who utilize research in neuroscience, cognitive development, biology, and other sciences to help us understand what a child's brain and body are capable of at different stages. Better yet are the experts who combine this scientific approach with real life experience as teachers, social scientists, parents, or therapists.

There are a number of books that have helped me understand what is at play in my daughter's mind, body, and nervous system at various ages. What I like about these books is that they don't push a parenting framework. Rather they give interesting insights into child development that enable us to make informed parenting choices. They've helped me understand what my daughter may be experiencing and have given her and I more common ground. For a full list of my book recommendations (and other resources), scan the QR code in the appendix or visit ScreenFreedRevolution.com/look-up-resources.

My master's degree is in Human Development and Education, so I love nerding out over development. But that's not why I've introduced the topic.

This is why:

Understanding where our children are developmentally can help us set appropriate expectations and even anticipate some of their behaviors, needs, and responses.

When our expectations for our children's behavior during travel don't align with their development, it's no wonder we scramble for the most effective way to occupy them: a screen. Whether it's a game, a drawing app, a TV show, or another captivating screen activity, we can almost always count on the device to generate the result we want: Still, quiet children.

One slight problem. Stillness and quiet are not the natural qualities of children, whose bodies and minds are primed for dynamic movement and activity that generates new neural pathways and important muscle groups. So how do we marry safety requirements and demands of polite society with the developmental needs of our children?

Check In:

What are your primary sources for knowing what to expect from your child's stage of development? How does it feel when you rely on external factual information as well as your internal guidance system?

Understanding Breeds Empathy

Love and Logic™ parenting philosophy teaches that every boundary should begin with empathy. They tout the importance of our children hearing empathy in our voices when we enforce a limit. But I think empathy has another important role. For me, empathy is the foundation of me being able to depersonalize my daughter's actions.

Have you ever felt like your kid is pushing your buttons? Have you wondered if children purposely ignore rules to see if they can get a reaction from us? Even when we know they're not breaking a rule or pushing a boundary to bother us, it's hard to not take it a little personally, especially when their behavior causes a mess or extra work for us. However, taking it personally is tied to a belief that they are doing these things *to us*.

True understanding of their developmental needs and capabilities is the way to wipe out the beliefs that lead to expectations that don't align with development.

Around the time LP turned 5, she started to hang on everything. She'd hang off the fridge door, the cupboard handles, the back of the couch, the towel bar, and often, some part of my body. I had just finished remodeling our house, and I lived in constant fear of the cracking and crashing sounds that would mean a drywall or cupboard repair. Over and over, I told her the damage she could inflict on these things that weren't meant for hanging.

Over and over, she nodded along and then proceeded to hang from everything she could wrap her hands around.

Then I read *Balanced and Barefoot*. The author, an occupational therapist, shares that kids' urge to hang is actually driven by development. Their hands are extra strong to enable them to hang from, well, anything. This hanging helps develop their shoulder girdle. Interestingly, strong muscles supporting the shoulder girdle are required to develop the smaller muscles in the arms required for fine motor tasks like writing.

My daughter was instinctively doing this seemingly random and to me, super annoying, activity that would support her future writing abilities in school—possibly even more than the Kindergarten readiness workbooks I'd purchased. Understanding that didn't make the fridge handles any less vulnerable, but it did help make my approach to the situation empathetic and solution-oriented.

I started taking her to the park more often, challenging her to see how many monkey bars she could cross, letting her dangle from my arms and shoulders (kids are the best free CrossFit workout), and pointing out more things she could safely hang from. As she got more appropriate opportunities to hang, she naturally followed the rules about where not to hang. It wasn't an overnight solution. However, armed with the understanding that she wasn't being a pill and was actually doing important work for her body, I was motivated to help her find solutions that worked for her development *and* our appliances.

When you have a grasp of your child's developmental capabilities, their behavior can take on purpose. It relieves our frustration or anger to know there may be a point to their behavior (or to know that they quite literally lack the brain function to choose differently). This seems to make it easier for our rational, adult minds to accept our kids' actions and meet them with a boundary based in empathy and/or a creative solution.

Check In:

If you want to interact with your child from a place of empathy, what fuels your ability to find that empathy? Conversely, what drains it?

Powering Creative Solutions

Toddlers' and young children's natural state is basically in opposition to the long waits and sitting periods of most travel. Now we know how to fuel empathy in these situations. Furthermore, when we understand a lot of their behavior comes not from naughtiness but from a misalignment of their developmental stage and the rigors of travel, we're more primed for problem solving. Even if we don't like their behavior, when we operate from understanding versus resistance, we can come up with creative solutions.

I tell LP all the time that a frustrated brain is not a creative brain. When we're annoyed by behavior we don't understand and don't like, it's hard to step back from our feelings enough to think of innovative solutions.

I once saw a Dad walking his toddler up and down the aisle on a Southwest flight. His son was delighted to be on-the-go and too busy grinning from ear to ear to make a peep. I've seen parents snag window and middle bulkhead seats to afford their child more room to stand, jump, and even practice karate in between the parents' seats. I've seen parents playing fetch with their children (yes, kind of like dogs) in empty parts of the bus, train, or airport terminals to burn off energy before take-off. More and more airports are adding play structures, giving kids a chance to climb, slide, and hang.

With better understanding of LP's developmental needs, I've also incorporated breaks into our road trips.

Pre-kid, I treated road trips like a personal challenge to beat the map's estimated arrival time. This didn't make me a super fun road-trip companion if you like to stop at spots of interest, enjoy the experience, or take care of basic needs like food and bathroom breaks. Though my road trips have inevitably involved more stops since attaining a tiny passenger, a couple years ago I fully gave up my racing ways and began to incorporate fun breaks.

LP and I now are known to stop at new parks, to pull over when a piece of nature looks particularly inviting, and to take stretching breaks. Even though I watch with disappointment as all the cars I just passed go zooming by, I have to acknowledge that both of us get back into the car after these breaks feeling refreshed, less tetchy, and friendlier to one another. I know of parents who make it a game to map out as many parks along the road trip route and do 10-minute mini visits to each.

Check In:

What creative solution have you come up with that met your child where they were? Can you take a moment to feel proud of that? Did the examples above spark any new ideas for you? Check out the Wild and Screen Freed Travel Families Facebook group for lots more tips.

CHAPTER 11

The Pre-Trip Groundwork: You

I
T'S KIND OF FUNNY HOW SO MUCH OF MANAGING OUR CHILDREN'S behavior actually starts with us. I've found that to be true for adults too.

Often, I find myself really wishing someone else would change their behavior, maybe that my partner would work out more, that my dad would call me more often, or that my best friend would quit the job she hates and pursue her "side hustle" full time. I want to motivate them to do those things—but how? I can cheer them on, remind them, nag them, or engage any other "motivation" that looks like me pushing or pulling them, but the result? It doesn't work well.

Instead, the most influential thing I can do is lead by example. When I am working out and hyped about it, my boyfriend often joins in. Calling my dad more often seems to remind him to do the same. Even something as monumental as a career change can be contagious. When I make a brave and bold leap (ahem, like writing a book), it seems to plant a seed for those around me to look at where they could bypass fear and jump.

This chapter is about how you can lead by example. How your perspective regarding travel will influence your child's. In order to do that, we're going to go through some misconceptions and unhelpful thoughts around travel (especially screen freed travel), clear out anything you wouldn't want to model, and make room for a flexible, fun, and free attitude.

Your Unshakeable Why

Why do you want to travel with your kids? For real, I'm asking this question. For some, the answer is simple: You love to travel. For others, the answer is layered or complex.

The primary reason my daughter and I travel is for our relationships. Our family lives in two places; one is a seven-hour drive away and the other takes about two hours to reach by plane. My closest best friend lives two hours away in another state. Several of my other best friends live in other states. We have to board a plane to see them. These spread-out friends are a casualty of being a wanderer in my youth and also meeting other wanderers; few of us stayed where we met.

Relationships are the most important thing in my life. LP and I usually go back to my hometown several times a year, which racks up at least 50 hours on the road annually. We try to visit our out-of-state best friends at minimum once per year and it usually ends up being more. Because of my flexible work schedule and since my daughter and I are a family of two (all my friends are families of four), it just makes sense for us to fly to visit them more often.

But we also travel for the love of it. Travel is how I found myself in my 20s. I quit an exciting job, sold my car and all my furniture, and moved to Ireland in 2009. Though, from an economic perspective, it was a terrible time to leave (whoops!), it was one of the most valuable things I've ever done.

I love being anonymous in a new place. Sitting in a cafe where everyone around me is speaking a language I can't understand is my jam. I enjoy masquerading as a local and imagining what it's like to live there.

I want to give my daughter a chance to catch that traveling bug. I want her to have an open, global perspective. I want her to have what I have—a network of friends who live all over the world who can offer me different perspectives and prevent echo chambers. I want not only for her to be unafraid of new, unfamiliar situations but to relish them.

I also want her to see that it doesn't take a lot of money to travel, and it certainly doesn't have to look a certain way. I want her to see fewer obstacles to travel and more reasons to make it happen.

These are all the reasons why we travel together. Maybe some of my reasons overlap with yours. Maybe not. It's important for you to identify why *you* want to travel with your child.

Like everything in life, a strong "why" will power you through material or internal obstacles and challenges.

Check In:

What's your reason for wanting to travel with your family? Get clear on this, because this reason needs to be more important than your reasons *not* to travel. It'll need to be more important than frustration, disappointment or fear when things don't go how you want them to during travel. Which leads us into our next tool for building a healthy travel mindset...

Travel is Messy

Travel is messy. If it's been a while since you took a trip, you may be glorifying how great it was. I certainly do this.

I remember the breathtaking beauty of the Swiss Alps, not the blazing hot hostel I tried—and mostly failed—to sleep in before visiting them. I remember the first time I looked out the bus window at Dublin rolling by and saw my last name on one of the street signs, not the night I showed up at my hostel after traveling all day to discover they didn't have my reservation or a room for me.

When I more honestly dig into my memories, I remember missed train connections, sprinting through terminals with my rucksack digging into my shoulders, getting lost, running out of money on the last day and having to survive on airplane snacks, and uncountable changes and challenges.

Bringing children along may exacerbate the potential for challenge or complexity, but kids don't create it. That's travel itself.

The more adventures we undertake, the more room for mess within the magic.

You may be asking, "What if something goes wrong?" The answer: It might. The truer answer: It probably will.

There is a universal law that no matter how well you plan, something will not go as expected on wedding days (spoken after a decade in catering) and during adventures. Plan on trips not going exactly according to plan.

When you can set out with the expectation that you may need to dodge or swerve at some point, you won't waste time being mad about it. Instead, you'll accept the mess and get on with finding a solution. Along the way, you'll model mental agility and emotional flexibility for your children. What an opportunity!

Check In:

Can you look back over your past travels and remember what went wrong? Can you also remember that sometimes the best times and surprise solutions come from things not going according to plan?

If you haven't traveled much, take a veteran traveler's promise to heart: Travel is messy. Acceptance of that fact will make the hiccups and halts far less upsetting and may even lead you to awesome, unexpected experiences.

Instagram Is a Liar

I could write a whole book on this topic, but I'll keep it short and sour this time. Instagram is not real. TikTok is not real. Facebook (I know, I'm aging myself as an Elder Millennial) is not real.

Rarely, do influencers put their children's tantrums or tough bedtimes into a reel. It's mostly happy faces staring out train windows, smiling families at delicious-looking international dinners, and for some reason, so, so many children wearing shades of beige (why??).

No social media video can capture the exhausting feat of carrying a sleeping toddler in your arms with a diaper bag on your back while steering an unwieldy luggage cart one-handed.

We may know this intellectually. But unfortunately, our bodies and nervous systems can still be fooled. Our bodies don't know social media isn't real. When your body is exposed to perfectly curated videos of idyllic and unrealistic travel, it accepts those as reality. Then, when your family's trip doesn't look like those videos, shame can start creeping in.

We can combat this in a few ways. And this isn't just for travel content; we can apply this approach to *all* social content.

After watching the video we can say out loud, *"That wasn't the full story. That is not reality. That is one tiny snippet of what happened, and though it is pretty and artistic and even moving, it is not real life. My trip won't be entirely like that, and it's okay."* This helps our body and nervous system adjust and categorize that pretty video where it belongs—in fiction.

We can also choose to unfollow, snooze, or scroll past without watching those types of videos, especially as we prepare for a family trip. We can seek out influencers who post the good, bad, and stinky of parenting to give ourselves a balanced perspective.

Either way, don't let Instagram be your guiding light for how you think your trip will go. Your trip will be your own. There will be magic during your family's adventure that no video could *ever* capture. There will be mess too. Both are part of travel.

Check In:

Can you think of social media accounts that you follow to "inspire you" but that really leave you feeling less than, left behind, or jealous? I'm a big fan of the "unfollow" button but if you don't want to go that far, then try the tactic above of reminding yourself that it's not real.

Give Yourself the Out

This is a tricky topic, and I say it to you as an eldest child and Type-A personality. The pressure to do the "right" thing (which actually means to do the thing my family expects of me) is *very* real. I don't take what I'm about to tell you lightly:

You don't have to go.

If you are preparing to take a trip that you feel is only meeting someone else's requirement or expectation, consider that you do not have to go.

Holidays, birthdays, funerals, weddings, bachelor and bachelorette parties, whatever the really valid and important reason someone else has for you to travel is *their* reason. If you don't have a compelling reason to go, or if the reasons *not* to are greater, you don't have to go.

Consider this your permission to disappoint someone else instead of disappointing yourself.

I like to say I am a major "show-er upper." This isn't just something I say though. I travel for my people, and I travel for their events. A majority of the flights I take each year are to visit loved ones or attend their life events. And yet, I have been willing and continue to be willing to disappoint them when I don't feel 100% in for traveling.

I've missed bachelorette parties, because I was pregnant or had a new baby. I've missed weddings, because spending the money to go would have put me way off-budget. I've stayed home for holidays—and here's the real growth point for me—simply because I *wanted* to. My family was disappointed. But I wasn't. Being in my home for that holiday felt right for me and my girl.

Now that I have a daughter there are all kinds of costs I factor in beyond money. The pros have to outweigh the cons of disrupting her schedule and missing things here at home.

I've also taken red-eyes to surprise friends; I've "gone ramen" for weeks to afford flights; I've driven eight hours through the night to see my family for 48 hours and then driven back. I sacrificed countless luxuries in my daily life to afford to move to Ireland when I was making $25,000 a year.

The point is that I will go to great lengths to travel *when I choose to*. I truly wanted to take those trips, so I was willing to pay the prices.

If your trip feels like an obligation, not a choice, your mindset is weakened before you even get out the door. If something goes awry on that trip, it will feel that much harder to deal with. It will also drain your capacity to stick to new screen habits. Your kids will pick up on and react to your lack of ease. You may find yourself blowing up at the people you traveled so far to be with. You may end up exhausted from staying up late just to feel like you've taken back some of your agency (bedtime procrastination, anyone?). You may not be able to enjoy activities and excursions, because they can't match the financial anxiety they're causing.

My best advice: Only take the trips you feel good about for your whole family (whether they travel with you or stay behind) and that align with the why you defined earlier in this chapter.

However, because this is real life, you might end up on trips you felt compelled—but not excited—to take. If you do, you can use what we learned in Chapter 9. You can shift to a perspective that may still allow you to appreciate the trip instead of dreading it.

First, acknowledge and feel your feelings. Allow thoughts like "I don't want to go. This isn't my preference. I would rather stay home. It's going to be a lot of work/money/time/emotional effort." Whatever reasons you have for not wanting to go are valid.

Once you have fully explored and felt those feelings, consider that you don't have to go, and if you do go, own the fact that you're choosing it. You may be choosing out of obligation or to fulfill a promise or to make someone else happy, but you *are* choosing it. Acknowledging that you are saying yes to the trip can give you a sense of empowerment instead of feeling like the victim of someone else's expectations.

Next, you can reframe the earlier thoughts about not wanting to go into a *two things are true* statement.

"I don't want to go because of <insert reason>. That is a valid reason. My feelings are valid. And I am choosing to go because of <insert reason>."

I often find myself saying this, "I wish my friend would come visit me, so I don't have to fly to her, because it's a pain to find and pay a dog sitter. My feelings about that are valid. And I know it isn't feasible for her family of four to come see us anytime soon. Spending time together is important to me, so I am choosing to go."

Check In:

Do you truly want to go on the trip you're considering? If not or if you're unsure, can you sit with those feelings? Then can you explore whether or not you really need to go? Lastly, if you don't want to go but you decide to anyway, can you work through the steps above to get to a *two things are true* statement that gives you a way to name your experience and perhaps find some peace?

Choose a Mantra

You know how the flight attendant says during their boarding spiel to put on your oxygen mask before you put on your child's? This is so important that, at least on Southwest flights, they come check in with every passenger accompanying a child to make sure they heard those instructions.

It's more than a sentiment. It's a practical approach to take care of yourself so you can take care of your little one. And yet, it's one of the most difficult things to implement. We are constantly faced with the challenge of "too little time, too much to do." The easiest response is to sacrifice ourselves and our needs to take care of our children. When it comes to travel, it's imperative to care for yourself (and maybe, just maybe, in every other area of life too).

This whole book is about equipping you with all the tools you need to travel screen freed with your family. Some of those tools are tangible, but as you've seen, far more are mental and emotional.

Another such tool is a mantra. I suggest creating a mantra that you can repeat to yourself, especially when you find yourself chasing a toddler down a terminal lugging two bags and pushing a stroller (I've done it), entertaining a preschooler in a boiling hot plane on the Phoenix tarmac during a two-hour departure delay (this too), running out of diapers while stuck in the air (unfortunately, yes), or driving for two hours with a crying toddler because there's a blizzard outside and the car heater only stays warm if the car is driving (lookin' at you, Volvo).

Did a mantra make all those problems disappear? Definitely not. But it was a way of caring for myself. It made the challenges more manageable by tying together all the work we did in this chapter.

A good mantra:

- Puts the focus on your WHY for travel
- Acknowledges the hard *and* the wonderful of where you're at with a *two things are true* statement
- Is yours and no one else's
- Reminds you that you chose this

My mantra is usually something like

- "Travel isn't easy, and it is worth it to give my daughter and myself new experiences."
- "I don't like that things are going wrong, and I am building important skills as I deal with them and modeling curiosity, problem solving, and flexibility for my girl."
- "This isn't for the faint of heart, and that's good, because I am strong."
- "This trip might be easier if my daughter had screen time, and I'm more interested in connecting with her than making it easy."
- "We want close relationships with our long-distance family, and we are willing to travel to see them."

A mantra can be as simple as "I love to travel, and my child will too." This is especially helpful if you've worked so hard to make this trip happen, and the little person you invited is complaining or being ungrateful.

A mantra can apply to the situation that is stressful:

- "Babies/toddlers/kids cry, and it's normal and okay."
- "This tantrum is embarrassing, and it doesn't mean anything about my child or my parenting."

For some people, the "and" mantra isn't necessary, and the best one is short, sweet, and focused on the positive.

- "This is worth it."
- "I'm proud of myself for doing this."
- "I can do this."
- "Look at us, we are traveling screen freed as a family!"

Travel takes us out of our comfort zones, and this may be hard for babies and young children to adjust to at first. Screen freed travel pushes us even further out of that zone. I can say, from the perspective of someone whose daughter is very well-traveled, it gets easier with repetition. Eventually it's not only *not* hard, it's something both you and your kiddo will look forward to with delight.

Pro tip: I'm notorious for coming up with an amazing mantra and then forgetting it the second my brain has to respond to stressful stimuli. For this reason, I usually write it down on a sticky note and put it in my jacket pocket or in my book as a bookmark. I have even made it into a cool graphic and made it my phone lock screen image. Keeping it handy enables me to use my mantra to take care of my emotional self before addressing my daughter's needs. I also say them out loud in front of her to model this tool of emotional validation and regulation.

Check In:

Have you ever used a mantra before? If not, practice using them in your daily life to see if they help. My mentor suggested "I'm doing my best" in a particularly tough season of parenting for me. It felt so affirming, like something I would say to someone else but hadn't considered saying to myself. A fellow author shared her mentor's mantra, "It's just right, so just write," and I've chanted that to myself an unbelievable number of times while writing this book.

Choose a mantra that feels kind and compassionate, the type of thing you would say to a loved one.

CHAPTER 12

The Pre-Trip Groundwork: Your Child

Y OU CAN MAKE SCREEN FREED TRAVEL EASIER BY DOING PREP WORK with your child. Especially important before a first trip or if your family doesn't travel often, these tips can be used over and over and modified as your children grow up.

When

How far in advance you tell your kids about the trip will depend on factors like their age, temperament, experience with travel, and capacity to deal with change.

I attended a weekend motherhood retreat with a woman whose son really likes routine. Changes to his routine are very disruptive to him, and she's found that he does better if he has a lot of time to prepare and is given many reminders. Two weeks before she left for our retreat, she told him she'd be gone for two nights. Every few days, she'd remind him it was coming and describe what would be different. He handled her departure calmly.

When my daughter was a toddler, I wouldn't tell her we were traveling until the day before the trip. If I told her farther in advance, she wanted to pack and leave right away. She'd wake up every morning thinking it was the day of the trip and be disappointed when it wasn't. Since we usually have early morning flights or road-trip departures, telling her the prior day seemed to give her enough time to get excited. By the time she next woke up, our adventure was beginning!

That worked then, but what works now is telling her a month in advance where we are going and who we will see. Even at 6, she still doesn't have a great concept of days and weeks passing, so she'll ask me to show her on our calendar where I mark our trips in purple. Then I'll give her a heads up when we're a week out. At that point, she begins a countdown, excitedly verifying with me every morning the number of days until we leave.

The evening before, I have her pack the things she wants to bring in her travel backpack, and we discuss how the next day will unfold. When she was a 2-year-old who couldn't pronounce "tr," she unwittingly created our family travel slogan, "We're goin' on a 'riiiiip!" We say this at least a dozen times while packing, and it's how I wake her up before we leave. It's our favorite travel tradition.

You'll find the right timeline for your kids. You know your child best. And if you learn through trial and error, that's okay too.

What/How

How you tell your child you're leaving and what you share about the trip will depend on a lot of factors. The amount of detail you give may vary.

One trip when LP was about 3, we were going to fly somewhere but we also had to use other methods of transportation. I told her we were going to drive our car to the parking lot, take a bus (from parking) then a train (to the terminal), and then a plane. We chanted car, bus, train, plane, car, bus, train, plane on the drive there. As we took each form of transportation, she noted it out loud, and we chanted what was left. Car, bus, train, plane. On every trip since, she asks me what kinds of transportation we'll be using and chants them to herself throughout the transfers. It seems to help her with the transitions.

Setting expectations for the transit time is tricky. Telling my daughter a flight or drive will take three hours means nothing to her. I try to find ways to put it into a perspective she can better grasp like "this drive will be longer than our last road trip but shorter than our drive to Mimsy's." Or "by the time you listen to five Jack and Annie chapters and have a snack, we will be getting ready to land."

For children brand new to travel, be sure to appraise them about what will be a new experience or things you think might challenge them. How you frame this matters. If you say it like a warning, they may interpret it as a bad thing. Try to be neutral and informative. It also helps to frame something positively, as long as you aren't b.s.ing them (have you noticed what great B.S.-radar children have?). Feel free to borrow from *Love and Logic*™ with a "Some kids ... " statement.

"Some kids feel like the plane ride lasts a long time, but other kids feel so excited to ride on a big airplane that it feels quick."

"Some kids like to pack a backpack of toys and coloring books to take with them. Does that sound fun to you?"

"Some kids find the airplane to be loud."

"Some kids feel their tummy do a somersault when the airplane takes off."

"Some kids like to be adventurous and try new foods when they travel."

"Some kids like to look for animals out the window while we drive and other kids prefer to color."

"Some kids never get to ride on a ferry/bus/train/plane. After this trip, you'll be able to tell them all about it!"

3 Types of Why

There are three types of "why" to travel that you might communicate to your child. I like to touch on all three but usually in different conversations with LP.

The Obvious Why

The Obvious Why is the reason why you are traveling. You can introduce this naturally during the "what" conversation. Is this trip based around an event, like a wedding? There's your Obvious Why. This why includes who you will see, a few things you plan to do, and what is special or interesting about the place you're visiting.

Remember: for tiny humans who are new to the planet, what is "special" doesn't have to be revolutionary. It could be as simple as "they have cactuses in Phoenix," "we might see deer in the forest," "Grandma has bunnies who live in her yard," "they eat something called paella and we'll get to try it," or "it will be <insert some weather or temperature they're not used to>." What is ordinary for us can be extraordinary for them.

Your Travel Why

The second type of Why is the one we already identified in the previous chapter: Your Travel Why. This can include why you love to travel or always wished you could travel, what you enjoyed about traveling as a kid or why you wish you'd traveled as a kid, and why travel is important to your family. This is a great conversation for reflecting on your family's values.

During my human development program, I read an article that stuck with me. It recommended storytelling as a way to communicate family values. In this way, parents create the family culture. I use the following conversation starter, "In our family, we ... " and then tell a story about it. Instead of being directive about our family's values, this phrase is inclusive and acts as an invitation for LP to be part of something greater than herself: our family's culture.

Here are a few of our "in our family" statements regarding travel:

In our family, our relationships with loved ones are our most valuable treasure. That's why we spend our time and money traveling to see them and why they do the same. (This communicates that in our family, love is about actions and those should flow both ways.)

In our family, we practice being present when we travel. (A way of framing the benefits of screen freed travel.)

In our family, we acknowledge the people we meet. (More effective than demanding that she wave or say hello.)

In our family, we are adventurous and we try new things! (This has been a powerful confidence booster and a call to brave new situations, even when she's been in developmental phases that make her not want to branch out!)

You can choose your own that help you communicate the values of your family. Much like a community, each family has its own culture and expectations for every member. The more open we are about these standards, the more we can invite our children into understanding what they look like as we practice them together.

◼ Your Child Why

The third and final why is my favorite, because I like to imagine the warm fuzzy feeling of being wanted that my daughter must feel when she hears this. This is the Child-Specific Why, and it's absolutely priceless. I recommend saying this out loud to your child whether they're 3 weeks or 13 years old.

Communicate to your child why you want her to be on this trip. What are you excited to share/do/see with her? What specific magic will your child bring to this trip that is unique to him? What do you enjoy about being with him?

One side effect of children's incredible ability to be in the moment is that they are quite observant. So I tell my daughter, "I'm so glad you're going on this trip, because you notice things when we travel that I would look right past. I'm excited for what you'll discover and share with me."

Other simple statements can be "I can't wait to do XYZ with you." or "I can't wait to show you XYZ and see what you think of it." "It'll be so special to see this new place alongside my favorite kiddos." "I wonder how your awesome good morning hug will feel when we get to London?" "Whether we're at home or on a trip, I am a super happy mama/daddy when I'm with you."

It's impossible to overdo this. Every human deserves to know that they are welcome and wanted. Imagine the self-concept of children who are shown the specific and unique ways they contribute to the world just by being alive. You can give your children this gift.

Make the Child the Expert

Imagine that you started a new job, and you were a novice at everything. You didn't know the typical stuff like where things are, who everyone is, or the internal company processes. But then imagine you also didn't know how to clock in or turn on a computer. Further imagine that you didn't know how to dress for the job, didn't have the right words to communicate effectively with your new boss or coworkers, didn't have the language to even begin asking questions to get the answers you need. Further, imagine the whole work environment was created for people who are 12 feet tall, so it was difficult to walk up the stairs, sit in chairs, use writing implements, drink out of coffee cups, and interact with your surroundings.

That's basically what it's like to be a toddler or young child.

They're new to everything! Due to their developing bodies and minds, they can be unsuccessful at their attempts to navigate our big, grown up world. Oftentimes, we find this charming and cute. But for them, it's not fun to always be the newest and worst at things adults do with ease. Their desire to master something must be intense.

That's why children love to be teachers of what they've learned. When my daughter begins a sentence with the words, "Mama, can I show you ... "

or "Mama, let me teach you ... " I do my best to drop whatever I'm doing and tune into her. She so often turns to me for instructions or help; I know she revels in the role reversal.

In travel, do your best to help your child be an expert.

Before your trip, think of how to equip them with knowledge about the mode of travel. For example, as my 2-year-old daughter and I prepared for several flights in early 2020, we read books about airplanes, looked for airplanes in the sky when we were outside, talked about the different simple features of airplanes like wings, the cockpit, the tail, luggage storage, the seats inside, and the pilots. When we got on the first flight, I pointed all these things out. That way, when we boarded to return home, she could point them out to me (to her delight and mixed reactions from the adults, she also pointed them out to many of the passengers boarding with us). She was thrilled to become a plane expert.

On our next flight, I suffered temporary amnesia and forgot what the cockpit was or the difference between wings and the tail. She reminded me of all those things, further solidifying her expertise in plane flying. She got to feel good at traveling because of her knowledge.

One of her favorite things to watch for are those wing flaps that come up during landing to help slow the plane. We call them wing brakes (I once looked up what they are called and it wasn't as cool as wing brakes, so welcome to my made-up vernacular). Every single landing, she has her eyes glued to the window to be the first to spot the wing brakes. She's the Expert Wing-Brake Spotter.

Furthermore, all this knowledge of what to expect took some of the unknown out of flying. It's easy to forget that routine is stabilizing for young children. Travel, of course, abolishes all of that. That's part of why we're doing it—to expose our children to more of the vast, beautiful world and give them opportunities to practice flexibility. But the novelty is also part of what can make travel challenging for children.

When children can disassociate from the discomfort of the unknown by disappearing into an app, game, or television show, it makes sense that their behavior seems to indicate that they're fine. They're quiet, heads down, paying attention to the captivating thing. But make no mistake, they're still feeling everything while also missing the opportunity to build fundamental life skills.

Our children don't need to escape. They need us to help them find what comfort they can in the unknown (and for us to hold space for how they feel, not teach them to numb it). Hearing about a concept like "airplane" from you, reading about it in books, and seeing it in pictures is one level of perception. Getting to see it in real life and experience the vast size, the loud noise, the soaring feeling, thrill of takeoff and landing—that's a deeper level of perception.

Laying that early groundwork can help them take ownership of what they perceive. They know the vast airplane size is important for fitting in all the people; they can guess the engine is what's making the loud noise; they've held a toy airplane and flown it through the air in the same way they are now soaring; they can come in for a landing and know that thunking sound is the wheels coming down so the plane can land and taxi to the gate. You can give them the language and understanding ahead of time to make sense of their flight experience.

That way, they don't need to avoid the experience by disappearing into a screen. Rather they can embrace it and as a result, gain confidence.

Ask Questions

Sometimes I'm so busy checking off my list of things to tell LP about a trip, I forget the most simple tactic: Ask questions.

No matter how tuned into our kids we are, we can't always anticipate the way their young minds will work. It's amazing the things we think they'll want to know about the trip versus what they actually want to know or are worried about. That's okay, because we don't have to anticipate everything as long as we remember to ask.

You can be really direct and ask, "How do you feel about the trip?"

Be sure to give your child time to answer. Try your best not to supply multiple choice answers if she doesn't respond quickly. If you can wait 10 to 20 seconds for her to consider the question and go inside her developing brain to dig up the answers, you'll have a chance to learn about her. It really is amazing what our children will reveal in response to an open-ended question rather than when given options to choose from.

Another great technique is to ask your child if he has any questions for you about the trip.

If he doesn't respond with much when you ask, I suggest leaving the topic alone for a bit and seeing if he brings it up again. Kiddos often need time to put words to their thoughts and feelings.

Be the Change You Wish to See

I wrote this chapter with the perspective that you're reading it before your child has ever traveled. If your family has traveled before, with or without screens, the information is just as applicable. However, if you used screens on the last trip and you plan to limit or exclude them all together on this trip, it's important to set up the new expectation with your child.

This can be a brief conversation if the change will be minimal, if the trip was a long time ago, or if they are already accustomed to screen limits in daily life. It may be a more involved conversation(s) if the screen limit will be a big change, if the child associates travel with getting increased screen time, or if there have been many trips with screen usage.

It's most important to make sure the change doesn't feel punitive. Your child hasn't done anything wrong to "lose screens." Focus less on what is going to be missing or different, and more on what it means for your family. You can guide the discussion with imagery around the whole family having their eyes on the world around them, being present in the new place, giving each other attention, and the other options for entertainment. You can discuss all your ideas for analog entertainment and ask for theirs too.

I'm a big believer in admitting where we went wrong to our children. When I have increased screen time with LP and realized that we needed to pull back from it, I've said something like, "I made a mistake in letting us spend too much time on screens. At the time, I did it because [insert your reason]. Now I've had a chance to think about my approach. It's better for our brains and bodies to have less screen time, and I'm going to make some changes around that. Here's what that will look like [share changes]."

If your child is very resistant, be prepared to model screen freed travel for them. This may mean putting your phone away unless absolutely necessary. When you do need to use it, you can communicate why, e.g. "I am looking up directions to our hotel now." "I am going to check us in for our flight, so we don't have to wait in a long line."

Even if your children aren't resistant to the screen time limits, consider modeling the benefits of screen freed travel anyway. Many of us can remember our parents acting out the "do as I say not as I do" maxim in childhood. This is your chance to grow past that and let your children know you're in it together. It's also your chance to find out what it feels like to fully embody your travel experience.

Pack a book, magazine, or an adult coloring book—something analog that you actually enjoy—or prepare some fun conversation starters. Download an Audible you can both listen to in the car or with headphone splitters for a public environment. A fun thing LP and I like to do is take turns making up a story. She starts the story, I tell the next part, she tells the next, and so on; I get big laughs if I make the character fart, break the rules, or get foiled like Wile E. Coyote—typical kindergartener-approved humor.

Pro tip: If you've already been practicing reduced screen time in normal life, it'll be easier to model while traveling.

For a long time, I tried to cut back on my screen time through sheer willpower. This didn't work. I'm a single mama and business owner; I often don't have the energy to fuel enough willpower to combat the addictiveness of devices. I finally identified three critical steps that changed my screen habits drastically. I've shared the three steps in a training called 3 Steps to Take Right Now to Reclaim Your Brain, Your Peace, and Your Freedom from Screens. You can get it for free by scanning the QR code in the Appendix of this book or by visiting ScreenFreedRevolution.com/look-up-resources.

Check In:

I'm sure you noticed, the tips above don't just make travel easier for parents. They're designed to help our children grow and flourish through travel. We don't travel just to see other places. We travel to see who we become as a result of visiting other places. Check in with yourself—have you acknowledged the incredible opportunities you're giving your children? Do that now, and feel free to literally pat yourself on the back.

CHAPTER 13

Making the Nervous System Less ... Nervous

OUR NERVOUS SYSTEMS AND OUR "THINKING BRAINS" ARE DISTINCT from one another. Our nervous system is made up of our brain and spinal cord (central) and the nerves that run throughout our body (peripheral). The job of the nervous system is to process information it receives from our sensory systems and body parts in order to quickly trigger appropriate responses.

However, it's not always the best gauge of "appropriate." The nervous system is primitive. It hasn't gotten the memo that we no longer live on saber tooth tiger-infested plains. So it doesn't always judge what is an appropriate response to the external stimulus of our modern world.

This is how we can find ourselves reacting disproportionately to a situation. Fight, flight, or fawn are primal responses of the nervous system. I want to emphasize that these responses are not bad. When the situation warrants them, they are designed to save your life. But they may not be warranted in response to your toddler saying "Mommy" 13 times without taking a breath. This is annoying, but not life-threatening, but our nervous system can sometimes respond as if it's a mortal danger.

All of us adults are walking around trying to cope with the world with prehistoric nervous systems. And so are our children! (The chaos makes more sense now, right?)

Many of the skills we've already learned (especially the 3-part Framework for Acceptance) can be used to help calm the nervous system. We can also teach them to our children! However, sometimes something jarring or overwhelming happens that causes the nervous system to get stuck in hyper-mode. Or a compounding effect takes place that strains the nervous system, such as all the environmental changes during traveling. When this happens, it's helpful to have tools to help reset the nervous system.

This chapter focuses on what parents and children can do to care for their nervous systems and reset when needed.

Pre-Party Outside

Nature is incredibly grounding for humans. For all our technology and civilization, we are still two-legged, opposable thumbing, prefrontal cortex-boasting animals. While we lay on Tempur-Pedic mattresses inside climate-controlled buildings, it's easy to forget that we have animal needs. One of these needs is time outside.

Our bodies and nervous systems crave the outdoors just as much as they did when we lived in caves. Children are especially connected to this awareness.

We experience countless benefits from time spent outdoors. If you want to learn more about these benefits, check out *Until the Streetlights Come On*. It's an excellent (and comprehensive) book by Ginny Yurich, founder of the *1000 Hours Outside* movement.

Some of the benefits most significant to travel include better sleep, decreased anxiety, lowered cortisol (stress) levels, improved ability to focus, and increased feelings of happiness. Get the whole family outside to take advantage of the nature effect.

I have found that the more outside time I infuse into our travels, the more my daughter is emotionally regulated and easygoing. Furthermore, I suggest bookending travel with outside time. This can be accomplished by prioritizing a family walk or alfresco dinner the night before an early departure or outside time the morning of a travel day with a later departure. I know it may sound like "one more thing" to add to travel preparations, but this one thing offers many rewards. If fitting it in feels tight, consider if there is something—cough, screen time, cough—that could be replaced with time outside.

Move It, Move It

While I have very rarely achieved "worn out" status of LP's near-boundless energy, I have seen the positive effects of her moving her body. I'm sure we've all noticed our children are more emotionally regulated, mentally flexible, and generally agreeable when they've had a sufficient amount of movement in the day.

Enter: Sitting still in a seat for long trips.

Sitting for extended periods is hard for children. It should probably be hard for all of us, as it's certainly unnatural. But some of us, myself included, have been trained by long hours of seated work.

The physical constraint of being strapped into a car seat, confined to a small seat, or being restricted from big movements or running can wreak havoc on a young child's nervous system. Restraint and constraint do not align with their body's needs, and their nervous system knows this. Some kids deal with this without much fuss, and others have a big response.

So what can you do? Of course, you can't avoid sitting entirely. The best alternative is to take every possible opportunity to move. For road trips, this means building in time for breaks. For planes and buses that require butts to mostly be in seats, give your children time before and after transit to move their bodies. On trains and ferries, take advantage of the aisles and space to walk when it's safe to do so.

A cool thing I've seen recently are children's play structures in airports. LP was thrilled about the play areas at the Portland, Oregon and at Seattle, Washington airports. I enjoyed watching kids climbing, sliding, and getting their wiggles out as well as playing together. You can research in advance to find out if your departure or arrival airports have kid areas. Even though travel is harried and there's a schedule to keep, 15 minutes of playtime can be a worthy investment.

While airports and bus, train, and ferry stations are not designed for children's play, there are many ways to let a young child be active in waiting areas. Walking back and forth, counting how many times they can jump in place, climbing in and out of a chair, and towing their own small suitcase are a few. If you have the time, I advise letting them walk as much as possible, even if it leaves you pushing an empty stroller. Have them carry their own small bag as well. This builds strength and contributes to their sense of independence and self-reliance.

If you get to know your home airport or station well enough, you may even discover fairly deserted areas that are ripe for running. At our airport, there's a third level above the terminals that is mostly empty. When I let her run amok up there before flights, LP is noticeably calmer during transit.

Press Reset on Adventure

If tension or potential conflict is mounting within your child, consider a nervous system reset. Our children's undeveloped nervous systems are why they seem to struggle with emotional and physical regulation more than adults (well, more than *most* adults) and can be overwhelmed by environmental triggers.

Resets aren't just for children. People of all ages can benefit from a soothed nervous system. A nervous system reset is phenomenal during any kind of travel, especially if your partner or child is getting worked up.

Examples of resets include:

Singing loudly—Choose a song everyone knows and really get into it. Extra points for silly songs. Humming is effective too. Obviously this is not a tip for shared public transit.

Dancing—Seatbelted dancing is a thing. See who can get the most creative with their dancing, even while strapped in. Extra points for fist-pumping or disco moves.

Hugs—Get in a hug that lasts at least 15 seconds to achieve the reset. Full body contact is better, but if the seatbelt sign is on, a side hug is better than none.

Kissing—A seven-second kiss has the ability to reset the nervous system. Parents, start smooching! A kid version of this might be getting silly and planting kisses all over their face while making loud kissy sounds.

Exercise—This one is tough in many travel circumstances but possible. Remember, even something that doesn't involve big movement, like squats, seated knee raises, or calf raises to tip-toe, can help relieve the nervous system and cause a dopamine (happy hormone) release.

Deep breathing—I find this works best for kids when combined with imagery. LP and I blow on pretend mugs of hot chocolate to do slow exhales.

We pretend to be sucking up a noodle or filling our belly-balloon to do long inhales.

Progressive muscle relaxation—We call this the tightening game. The whole family can play! Everyone takes a deep breath in and tightens one body part as much as possible and holds it. Then let the muscle relax with a big out-breath sigh. Tightening the butt muscles usually gets a laugh from the kinder crowd.

Cross body activities—Movements that require our hands or feet to cross the centerline of our body can reset our nervous system as well as re-engage both sides of our brain. Think patty cake or opposite hand to opposite foot touches.

Chewing ice—The cold and crunchy nature of the ice can provide an effective sensory diversion.

CHAPTER 14

Destination Boredom

B OREDOM IS A CRITICAL OPPORTUNITY FOR OUR CHILDREN. YOU'RE about to find out how interesting boredom can be! In the following sections, discover what you can give your child that they won't get from the world, why young children are primed for self-entertainment, how to avoid training them out of this skill, and what to do if you already have (don't worry, it's fixable).

The Most Fascinated People on the Planet

When it comes to self-entertainment, very young children have something we don't: they're brand new to this planet. All we've seen and done every day for years is mysterious and marvelous to them.

Young children's newness, their proximity to the ground, and their propensity for wonder mean they see things we don't. And they're fascinated – like stopping in their tracks 15 times on a two-block walk fascinated – by what they see. They are born inherently creative, curious, and connected to the present moment. This makes them brilliant at being entertained by much less stimuli than adults.

When she was 6 months old, my daughter became obsessed with a Smartwater bottle. Dozens of expensive toys, and LP was all-in on something she found in the recycling bin. When that water bottle emerged from the diaper bag or she came round a corner to see it lying on the ground, it was as if all her dreams had come true. She'd get so excited she would practically vibrate. I kid you not, baby LP took her first steps in pursuit of that Smartwater bottle.

It's not just my daughter. The stimuli needed to entertain babies and young toddlers is very basic. Have you ever seen a baby staring enraptured at a ceiling fan?

If they're born with the capacity to be entertained by the environment of normal life lived around them, the good news is we don't have to teach them to enjoy the everyday world. It's simply our job to ensure we don't train it out of them by offering them too much high-stimulation entertainment.

The Case for Slow

Our job is to give tiny humans as much space and non-rushed time as possible. When they are focused on something, even if it seems meaningless to us, we can let them be. Better yet, we can come alongside them and also gaze at the trail of ants or whatever has caught their attention.

Having a baby or toddler is the greatest excuse that exists for slowing down. Yet, instead of joining them in their pace, we often sweep them into ours like a tornado pulling everything around it into its spinning vortex.

I get it. There is so very much to do. We sigh at the "nap when the baby naps" advice of older women. We can't see how to go slow *and* meet the demands society has placed on us—this culture of snap-back, sleep training, six-week maternity/no paternity leave, and baby nurseries that must look like Pottery Barn ads.

As a recovering tornado-mother, I implore you: if *you* can't go slow, at least try to give your little one the space to move at their unhurried, brand new human pace.

The world will teach them how to be fast-paced.

Busyness is one of the highest expressions of worth in Western culture. Public schools will move them from subject to subject in 50-minute intervals. Texting and emails have made letter-writing obsolete. Inventors introduce new technology, and consumers immediately demand they make it faster. More is more, baby, and more than that is better. Everything in our world is harried and hurried.

The smartphone plays right into this rushed worldview. Whatever we want is right at our fingertips all the time. Our questions, requests, and solutions are a Google search away. Escape from life only requires one swipe. We have found a small device that enables us to avoid … well basically everything, even something as integral to human existence as waiting. Except, not quite.

There are things we will never be able to rush. There are waits we cannot escape. Real friendship. Pregnancy and childbirth. Deep thinking. Not settling for the person in front of us and seeking the right partner. Learning a trade. College. Earning a promotion. Building muscle and endurance.

Some of the most meaningful human experiences require patience and fortitude. You can help equip your child to experience them by not investing in the currency of hurry.

Check In:

Where have you felt rushed since becoming a parent? Where did that feeling come from? What do you feel compelled to squeeze in? Can you practice considering whether something matters or whether you could let it go in favor of slowing down?

Opt Out of Filling All the Hours

Working parents are with their awake children for about 44 hours each week and stay-at-home parents are in for about 84. That's a lot of time to fill!

I love spending many of those hours engaging my daughter. Our favorite things to do together now that she's in kindergarten are reading, riding bikes, doing yard projects, cooking and baking, telling stories and jokes, and having dance parties.

But those activities don't account for 84, or even 44, hours worth of time weekly. Even if I wanted to, I couldn't devote all those hours to entertaining her and manage to complete house projects, run errands, pay bills, and fulfill my duty as provider, protector, and caretaker. It's impossible. Likely, you feel the strain of all you need to do on top of the awake hours your child needs a caretaker.

Thus, we have two choices. We can exhaust ourselves trying to plan activities, sensory bins, busy boards, art kits, and scavenger hunts, or we can turn on screens in pursuit of "keeping the kids busy."

Or we can not.

When we are willing to consider that our children can (and should, from a developmental perspective) find their own ways to fill many of those hours, we find our use of screen time as a babysitter reduces dramatically.

We can excuse ourselves from the belief that entertaining our children is our job. We can toss out the belief that boredom is harmful for kids. We can choose to believe that those times when kids are not externally entertained are *opportunities*. We can allow self-discovery and self-led play to be their training ground for:

- Building coping skills that foster emotional regulation
- Utilizing and strengthening the prefrontal cortex by engaging in planning
- Developing self-confidence as they navigate play without a parental safety net
- Exercising creativity
- Building self-reliance and autonomy by making their own choices
- Fostering curiosity, ingenuity, and problem solving

This isn't "outsourcing parenting to the child" or "shirking parental duties" as I've seen it referenced in online comments. It's giving kids the space to use the innate wisdom of childhood. It knows what their minds and bodies need. It's also a juicy gift of insight into our children's minds when they show us exactly what they are going to do about being bored (there's a story in the next chapter about this).

We want our children to have rich, full lives, so it reasonably seems like the path to more of that must be more of all the other "stuff" too. We keep thinking that it's about finding the right game, the perfect hobby, or the best enrichment activity that will entertain our child. We do it with the best of intentions. But what if *doing less* is the key?

Though we live in a "more is more" society, in the case of our young children, consider less is more. Or if we're looking for more, how about pursuing more of the following:

- Free, unplanned time
- Quiet environments
- Space to roam, preferably outside
- Play with other children that is not directed by adults
- Time to continue the activities that absorb them (even if they seem pointless to us)
- A gentle, "Not now" when they ask for screens
- A caregiver who models his or her own downtime and recreation

All Aboard the Boredom Train

Once you're on board with being bored, it's ideal to give your kiddo opportunities to practice before traveling. If you don't have much time before your next trip, that's okay too. Screen freed travel is a great training ground too, because it's unlikely you can pack enough non-digital items to keep them entertained the whole time.

At some point on the trip, your child will not be entertained with an official activity. Some of you feel uncomfortable thinking about that. I get it. But the sooner you can accept this as your travel reality, the happier you'll be.

Sometimes when we travel, my daughter brings a baby doll and spends 30 minutes putting it in and out of its airplane seatbelt or telling it about all the passing road trip scenery. I love those trips and have even gotten to read a book to the sound of those metal clasps clicking and unclicking. Other times, she blows through every book, coloring book, snack, and toy in the first 45 minutes. On these trips, there comes a time when she makes it clear that she wants something more to do.

If my goal was to keep her entertained for the whole transit time, I might then turn to a screen with its practically infinite options for diversion.

This is the point where mindset matters so much. Because I don't have the belief that I need to provide entertainment for the whole travel time, I am comfortable with her being bored. Thus, screen time doesn't even occur to me. Okay, it *occurs* to me, but it's just not a viable option for us.

On the trips when her entertainment bag didn't last (which is many of our trips) when she was a young toddler, I helped entertain her. We looked through the airplane safety manual to find babies (can you find all three on the Southwest manual?), we stared out the window to see if we could see animals or cloud shapes, and we talked. Sometimes it was mentally draining for me. Sometimes she was still bored.

That was okay. We were okay, because I am committed to the following:

- My daughter building vital life skills that don't involve being entertained by screens
- My daughter traveling with me and developing a love for it

Here's the funny thing about screens: We think they are making our jobs as parents easier. But they only make that one moment easier.

In reality, screens are stealing the opportunities from our children to learn the kinds of skills that actually make parenting easier in the long-run. Screens provide mostly passive entertainment that starts and stops with the device. Letting kids be bored and figure out what to do with it enables them to take an active role in their entertainment and build skills that last their entire childhood (and lifetime).

This is the difference between our kids seeing entertainment as consumption or entertainment as creation. There's room for both, of course, but not if the consumptive kind of entertainment is so excessive it shuts down a child's desire or ability to create.

For example, by teaching my daughter when she was young how to find entertainment using her environment (especially things that aren't toys), her imagination, her own body, and her five senses, I set myself up for an older kiddo who can do this stuff on her own. LP knows entertainment is available to her no matter where she is or what she has, because the only tool she really needs is her imagination.

Now that she's in kindergarten, we have entire flights and hours of road trips during which she colors, listens to an Audiobook, sings to herself, and plays make-believe with anything she can find as characters—her hands, a cup, a napkin, or stuffies or figurines she has brought. She mutters their voices as her fictional narrative unfolds. By herself. I'm happy to talk to her, and we still interact during transit. But she is not dependent on me, or a device, to entertain her. I read books on planes, listen to audiobooks, or do work, pausing occasionally when she wants to talk to me or share a snack.

As I've stated a few times in this book, this isn't because my child is exceptional. Neurotypical children (and plenty of neurodivergent children) are capable of this if they are given opportunities to practice and aren't taught that entertainment equals passive consumption.

As a traveling family, I can think of no better magic than looking over at your child who is staring dreamily out the window, lost in her own thoughts. Or when a half hour's silence in the car is broken by your toddler shouting, "Ten!" and you realize he's been silently counting wildlife he sees out the car window.

You Have to Board First

We don't just rescue children from boredom with devices; we rescue ourselves too. Next time you're in a waiting room, consider staying off your phone and observing the world. Watch how quickly people pull out their phones after they sit down (in my informal studies, it's either immediately or they already have their phone in their hand before sitting). The average person picks up their phone 352 times per day, according to the tech care company Asurion. What's really wild is this is a nearly 4-fold increase from 92 times per day in 2019 (only five years ago!) when Asurion conducted a similar study.

We know we have technology as a way to escape boredom for ourselves and our children. It would be crazy to deny that it exists and can be effective.

But it's not the *only* option.

We know this, of course. But how often do we behave like screens are the only option? How often is a smartphone the first and only way we seek to pass downtime or waiting?

In your quest to reduce or eliminate screen time while traveling, could you practice the same in regular life too? One thing I always recommend is to have a go-to list of entertainment options (for yourself or your children) that you try first. When I find myself waiting somewhere, I try three ways to amuse myself before I turn to my phone. Some analog ways to wait include:

Brain food—Reading for entertainment or learning is a great way to pass the time. I have one physical book and one audiobook in rotation at all times. Crosswords, Sudoku, and puzzles are not only great time-passers, they're linked to a reduced risk of dementia later in life.

Three deep belly breaths—I'm talking shoulders back, eyes closed (if it's safe), breathing slow and deep all the way down to your transabdominal muscles. Take as much time as possible. You spend hours of your day doing for other people; you and your body deserve these seconds.

Five senses—This also works as an anti-anxiety tool. Acknowledge five things you see, four things you can touch, three things you hear, two things you smell, and one thing you can taste. This little somatic trick helps us root right down into the present moment.

Best day ever game—I imagine how my day could go ridiculously, absurdly right. As in: no wait at school pick-up, my daughter races into my arms with joy as her teacher tells me I'm the best parent she's ever known, then I return home to a materialized chocolate cake, a perfectly clean house, and a self-cooking kitchen. We spend so much time catastrophizing and picturing the worst case scenarios. Why not put our imaginations to work imagining best case scenarios?

Organize your purse (or the front seat if you're in a drive-thru)— Sometimes I think being a grown up just means constantly sorting through and throwing away receipts. Anyone else?

Walk around—If my place in line is held and there is space for it, I walk around. We already talked about how movement is good for our children's minds and their bodies, and we're no different.

Talk to a stranger—My introvert readers may pass on this one. It's not for everyone, but I love to talk to other humans. Maybe it's the anonymity factor, but I find these conversations often go deep quickly. Some have even been life changing. One hundred percent of them were only possible because I was off my phone.

Sitting still—I know, I know. How on earth are busy parents supposed to accomplish all we need to if we are doing nothing? If I attempt to fully answer that question, this book will double in length. I'll just say this: We're human beings, not human doings. Sitting still gives us a chance to check in with the being part.

Our relationship to patience isn't fixed. It's a quality we can choose to strengthen. We're not aiming for perfection; we're seeking awareness of how we feel in the face of boredom and acknowledgement that we have other choices. Then, we practice.

Check In:

What is your relationship to boredom? Notice when you start to feel it; how difficult is it to avoid pulling out your phone? What different habits are you willing to practice when you have to wait or find yourself feeling bored?

Boredom Training Ground

There are a variety of ways to help kids learn to deal with stillness, quiet, "doing nothing," and being allowed to figure out how to spend their time. For example, "The Pause" from *Bringing Up Bebe*, a book all about Parisian parenting, begins when babies are infants.

Patience training is an effective exercise and simple to pull off. It goes like this: When a child asks for something, acknowledge them with eye contact and say, "I will do that. Please wait." Then turn away and do something else for a few seconds. Turn back to the child and say, "Okay, I'm ready to do what you asked." You may choose to note the way they waited, "I saw that you were calm and quiet while waiting." There's no need to heap on praise or thank them for waiting. Gradually you can extend the time of waiting until the child will wait patiently for a couple minutes.

We can model patience out loud. In line for something, we can say, "I don't really like to wait. I could get on my phone and take myself away from here. But I'd rather stay here with you, so I'll leave it in my pocket." Then amuse yourself in whatever way you need to pass the time.

Try to have more low-stimulation toys than high-stimulation ones. During my child development class in grad school, I read a study that indicated the more lights and sounds a toy has, the less a child has to engage their brain to play with it. That's just a toy with lights and sounds. Imagine how little effort a child's brain puts forth to watch a TV show.

Consider that no toys are needed. Throughout history, children have defied parent expectations and ignored the toy in favor of ... whatever was lying around. Shoes, blankets, pots and pans, and the box the toy came in have long-been favorites. This responsiveness to the items naturally around them is actually important to children's development. They're watching you navigate the world, and they want to be part of what you do. From a young age, they're naturally happier helping you cook or do chores than they are playing with the world's most awesome toy alone.

Speaking of development, children under 2 don't really get bored. So they don't need training to be curious or investigate their environment. But they do need experiences in the tangible, analog world, not the digital one.

Baby and toddler brains are primed to learn from observing but most importantly *physically interacting with* the three-dimensional world around them. They learn from the things they can touch and move through space. Two dimensional screens don't register in their brains in the same way as three-dimensional objects and the sensations that come with them. Despite the infinite range of topics, learning apps are, for the kind of input toddlers need, less effective and more risky than handing them a pot and wooden spoon.

For kids of all ages, the best boredom training is leaving them alone. Of course, I don't mean you should leave the house or completely ignore them. But I do suggest giving them the space to find something to do. If they complain of boredom, you can empathize, "Ooo, I know what it's like to feel bored. I've felt that way too."

The more you can help them gain the skills of patience, self-entertaining, and interest in simple things, the easier your travel with them will be. And don't worry, I've got your back with a magical question to support this process in the next chapter.

It's Not Too Late—A Tale of Neuroscience

It's almost never too late when it comes to children's minds. All humans' brains have neuroplasticity, which is a fancy way of saying that our minds and habits can be changed. In children, this plasticity is even more present. Childhood is a growth state that requires kids' brains to be extra adaptable.

If you have already instilled habits in your child like continuous adult-sourced entertainment or using screens to relieve boredom, I have great news. You and your child *can* learn new habits and ways of operating! It's 100% possible.

A few tips for reengineering your family's relationship to boredom and/ or screen time:

Don't expect it to suck. It's quite possible that the transition away from screen overuse could go smoothly. I cannot tell you how many parents I've worked with who have significantly reduced screen time or cut it out altogether, and their kids didn't really care. A lot of children know intuitively that they don't want screens, but they aren't going to set their own limits. They need us to do it. Same thing goes for giving them space to self-entertain.

Even if you feel sure your kid is going to freak out, try to keep an open mind. Remember, those mirror neurons are firing, and your child will often follow your lead. Make sure the contagious attitude you spread about these new habits is positive.

Don't just take away screen time or you as the entertainment source and expect your kids to deal with it. The longer they've had a lot of screen access or the longer you've made it your job to entertain them, the more support they may need in navigating the new way of life. In the beginning, consider replacing screen time with another offering. If your kids are used to getting on iPads after school, let them know that post-school time is now outside bonanza time! They can do anything they want in the backyard! Be sure to check in with yourself in case you have a belief that says less screen time has to mean more You-as-the-Entertainer time—it doesn't! (We dig into this more in the next chapter).

Decide whether you're going cold turkey or will gradually introduce new analog habits. I've seen the cold turkey approach work better for families, but some parents swear by slower change. You know your family. You choose. But whatever you choose ahead of time is yours to stick with. If it gets bumpy—if kids who are used to morning television or post-dinner video games are struggling to adapt to the changes—stay the course. The more steady you are, the quicker your kids can navigate to calm.

Arguably the most important piece of advice I have is to talk to your kids about why you're making these changes. Nobody, kids included, likes to be the subject of unexplained mandates. Discuss with your kids about what you've learned and how it has affected your parenting choices. When parents change their minds and own their growth as humans, we give our children permission to do the same. This kind of open dialogue models traits like humility, anti-perfectionism, critical thinking, and conscious decision making. It also equips them to make informed choices when they're old enough to manage their own screen time.

CHAPTER 15

The One Best Question

I CLOSED MY LAPTOP WITH A SNAP. (DOES ANYONE ACTUALLY CLOSE THEIR laptop slowly or gently?) I groaned slightly as I stretched out tight back muscles and walked out of my office. Where I was halted abruptly by an unfamiliar scene.

There were BRIO train tracks stretching the length of the hallway with figure eights running under bridges. Trains in various stages of travel sat on the tracks. A Cabbage Patch baby sat in a slumped reign over a small herd of what I can only assume were meant to be a My Little Pony version of wild horses. I followed the tracks down the hallway and into my 4-year-old's bedroom. Here, Calico Critters of all creeds could be seen undertaking various lifelike activities; skunks sat at a table awaiting pizza from the miniature pizza oven, mama squirrels stood over baby squirrels in strollers, a panda family seemed to be mid-stroll through a park composed of the wooden green BRIO pine tree silhouettes. Adjacent to the pizza parlor, a rabbit mom and baby enjoyed tea with Thomas the Tank Engine, another My Little Pony, and a National Forest doll.

My daughter, crouched on her haunches in the way young bodies naturally can, glanced up at me momentarily. Then she went right back to setting up the wonderland that had not long before been three bins of toys in her closet.

I gaped at two things: the speed with which she had set it all up and the proof that children left to their own devices contain within them infinite capacity for creation and world building.

The scene I was viewing was the answer to a question I had posed to my daughter about an hour earlier. I had been finishing some client work when she strode into my office, tapped me on the shoulder, and announced she was bored.

Often, the worst moments of parenting are born from those times when we have little capacity. That's when I snap more, give too many commands, and listen too little. But sometimes, great moments of parenting are born when we have too little time or energy to be the parent society keeps telling us we have to be: the one who always has entertainment set up for our children.

It was this way for me. On that day, I needed more time to finish a work project. I was frustrated that it had taken longer than the school day. I simply could not stop what I was doing to help solve LP's boredom problem.

I turned to LP and said, *"Oh. What are you going to do about that?"*

Now, surveying the realm she had created that spanned more than 20 feet and 30 characters, I had my answer.

This is what she did about feeling bored.

Not wanting to break the magic spell of her creativity, I slipped away to cook dinner and had to call twice to get her to come eat when it was ready. She was deep in a civilization of her own making.

This isn't always her response to that question. Sometimes she whines even more. But mostly, she figures it out.

I consider this type of situation to be a training ground—for both of us.

I polled parents to see how they feel when they sense their child is getting bored or when their child complains of boredom. Many of them said they have an urge to do something about it. They told me it's not the boredom they're really afraid of. They fear what boredom can lead to—whining, tugging on them, huffing, more whining, and eventually, a tantrum.

This is reasonable. Why steer into a tantrum when they have a tool to instantly navigate around it? Turn on the iPad, LeapFrog, or phone and *voila!* tantrum averted. Technology, viewed this way, is a tool to achieve a momentary calm during boredom.

But what if we stop treating boredom like it's a problem?

Boredom and waiting are natural parts of life and often the place where the most brilliant ideas emerge. The real thing we should be afraid of is what happens to children who haven't had a chance to face boredom? What if using technology to foster that "momentary calm" is actually preventing our kids from developing important skills?

So where do we get the belief that we need to entertain our kids? Why do we think we need to source activities for their enjoyment or that we should sate their need for diversion? In fact, why do we think that life is something from which we need to be diverted?

Check In:

What happens in your body and mind when your child complains of being bored? How do you usually respond? Is your response geared to relieve yourself of that feeling or help your child develop coping skills?

Turning Down the CEO Role

In this age, many parents are exhausted. We're running ourselves ragged, shuttling to and from countless kids' events and activities, planning Pinterest-worthy birthday parties, and coming up with a continuous slew of ways to entertain our kids.

I find myself wanting to shout from the rooftops, "This can actually be easier."

I understand why parents keep pushing so hard to enrich and entertain their children. It's an unspoken expectation that has become the norm in the last two decades. They don't want them to miss out on what the other kids have. They don't want to "fail in their parenting duties" to give their kids every advantage in a competitive world. Unfortunately, when they try so hard to entertain their children to prevent them from even the risk of being bored, two other things happen instead.

First, all the adult-driven inputs train children's brains to need more varied or exciting stimuli to get into play mode. Because they're just consuming the entertainment, not generating it, they will stay captivated for less and less time. This is a natural law; human minds and bodies are actually built to be less sensitive to stimuli over time. It'll take more effort to entertain them for less time. Imagine hearing the same joke over and over. Will it be as funny the third or or eleventh time you've heard it?

Second, parents trap themselves in the role of Chief Entertainment Officer, or CEO. This forces children to be dependent on parents, rather than themselves, for entertainment. A downside of falling prey to the myth that you are your child's CEO is you'll quickly find that their brilliant minds and energy-filled bodies are nearly limitless. If you're schlepping entertainment, they'll gobble it up and immediately ask for more. And more. And more. That only works in an ideal world in which parents have unlimited time, energy, and availability.

What about when you don't?

There will be a time (okay, thousands of times) when you simply don't have the capacity to think up and execute creative ways to entertain your children. When you are driving in traffic or juggling luggage through an airport. When you have a second child or a third. When your job gets demanding, you have to move, a loved one dies, you have health issues, or you want to train for that marathon.

It doesn't even take major life changes to deplete a parent's capacity. Stress, hunger, thirst, lack of sleep, and demands of regular life can add up and reduce what you have to give. Even something like having an uninterrupted conversation with your partner or a friend will give you less time to focus on entertaining the kids. Have you ever tried having a conversation with another adult only to be repeatedly interrupted by your children or theirs making demands or requests?

So when life happens and your capacity dwindles, what happens? If your children are used to being entertained by you, they may, justifiably, react to the change in attention with whining, tears, and other emotional responses. Obviously, this isn't fun to deal with when we're already short on capacity to begin with. How does that normally go in your house?

I'll speak for myself. In these situations, I don't act like the parent I want to be. I'm not even close. At my worst, I may yell or snap at my daughter. At best, I become a grumbling cave creature who resents everyone.

Many therapists and parenting coaches make the case for using screen time in these situations. In the immediate moment of choosing between giving your kid a screen for entertainment or losing it on them, I agree!

But handing them a screen only treats the momentary symptom—the fit or whining for attention—rather than the root problem. The real issue is that the child has been trained to seek entertainment from her parents, instead of from herself. Luckily, if this has happened to you, you can choose to help turn your child into her own Chief Entertainment Officer. That way, when your capacity is depleted, you don't have to extricate yourself from the CEO role. You've already hung up your hat, so to speak.

To start, you'll need to train yourself out of the mindset that you are your child's entertainer. You'll also need to unlearn that boredom is something to be rescued from, which we discussed in the previous chapter. This mentality is relatively new. You most likely don't need to undo generations of CEO parenting.

The typical Millennial childhood was like mine. I remember hours each day after school spent apart from my stay-at-home mother. Almost every evening when dinner was ready, she'd have to call me in from the trampoline, out of a tree, back from the neighbor's barn, off my bike, or away from whatever book world I'd disappeared into. But it's not the same for our children. Would you agree that we give them way less space, autonomy, and responsibility for their time than we had as kids?

After your mindset shift has occurred, you're free to support your child as she practices patience, self-reliance, creativity, and all the skills we've been discussing.

Life, especially for parents, is constantly shifting. As it does, our ability to entertain our kids will fluctuate. Wouldn't it be nice if your children were already in charge of much of their recreation time? Everyone benefits when we help our children master the art of self-entertainment. That way, parents and children can release the entertainer-audience dynamic and settle back into their natural relationship.

Back to the Magic Question

Try this at home before trying it during travel. Repeatedly, if possible.

Unless you are willing to try new things under totally unpredictable circumstances like some kind of a cowboy-parent, I don't suggest you quick draw, *"Ah, what are you going to do about that?"* on a bored child who's never heard it before. This might act like a wild west pistol whip and shoot holes in your plans for calm or regulated travel.

After you've practiced the one best question in day-to-day life a bit, it can be an incredible tool during travel. But only if you use it properly.

"You're bored? What are you going to do about that?"

Experiment with asking the question with genuine curiosity or cool, calm indifference. Trying saying it as a teammate would, as their biggest fan would say it. Or ask as if you can't wait to find out their answer. All of these are great options. Whatever you do, *don't* ask it with snark or blame in your voice. This is not a sarcastic response. It's actually a question with a real and valid answer.

Then wait. They may take a while to answer or to show you their answer. Keep waiting.

When LP was a baby, I received the golden advice to always wait for a count of 10 after asking her a question. Too often we adults interrupt children before they can answer. Or after a micro-pause, we rapid-fire a list of possible answers for them to choose from.

When we don't give a child time to process and respond, we miss out on the beautiful offerings of her mind. It takes time for these new little humans to decipher and consider the question—and they *will* consider it with surprising seriousness—and choose their answer. It's worth the wait, because inside that answer is a gold mine. It can tell us so much about our children, about their interests and values, about how they see the world, and about their innate creativity.

I actually count to 10 seconds slowly in my head.

The ideas LP has shared have surprised and thrilled me, even in an environment as contained as an airplane or car. I've had to say no to some of them ("I'm going to jump on the seat to see if it's bouncy like a trampoline." "I'm going to play some music, so the whole airplane can have a dance party.") But most of them lead to unforgettable experiences curated entirely by her, not me. All because of one simple question.

I can't wait for you to see how your child responds to this question. Just don't give up if the first few times don't take. We can't always conjure magic on a first try, but you and your kiddo will get there.

Check In:

What's your immediate response to the idea of this question? Compare that to what happens when you practice it.

CHAPTER 16

What to Pack and How to Rock it In Route

I TRIED NOT TO INHALE THE POOP-SCENTED AIR. THE AIRPLANE BATH-room seemed smaller than it ever had before, as I contorted to reach the tiny trash door and shove in LP's very full diaper. (BTW, airlines don't want you to do this. If you have a poopy diaper, you're supposed to ask the flight attendant for a plastic bag or bring your own. I learned this fun fact when I emerged from the bathroom—when it was already too late).

This was the third diaper change of this trip, a new travel record I hoped never to beat. LP hummed to herself on the tiny, fold-down changing table. I smiled, briefly thanking the stars that she held still for diaper changes.

I reached into the diaper bag for another diaper. My fingers touched the wipes, a plastic Puffs container, the round head of a Cabbage Patch baby, a container of snacks, my water bottle, and ... nothing else. There was no soft, cloth-like texture of a diaper. I frantically felt around again.

Panic set in. I started to sweat.

I dumped the contents of the backpack into the tiny airplane sink. No diaper. I ransacked the diaper bag pockets like a rubbish-raiding raccoon. No diaper. I counted out loud: one change in the terminal (almost causing us to miss family boarding), one change as soon as the seatbelt light switched off, and this change. Three changes, three diapers. My child had already pooped more in one day than she normally did in a week. And I, accustomed to several-day stretches without number twos, had woefully under-packed diapers.

I briefly considered wrapping her entire bottom half in several rolls of airplane toilet paper. You know that stuff that's the consistency of cardboard and the effectiveness of something only slightly more substantial than air? I quickly scrapped that idea.

The plane would begin its descent soon. We didn't have to wait long before we'd be reunited with the suitcase diaper supply.

Could I wing it?

Could this tiny human possibly contain any more diaper-filling surprises?

This was only our second flight. Back then, I was still trying to be an unobtrusive flier, still attempting to convince myself and the world that I wouldn't take up any more space, make any more noise, or be any more inconvenience than I had been without a child. Ah, silly, innocent, younger me.

Now, as a six-year-mom veteran, I would have marched up and down the aisle until I located a family with a comparably sized child and asked to borrow a diaper. Or I would have gotten one of those plastic bags from the flight attendants, bored two leg holes into it and put it over my daughter's onesie but under her leggings and sweater. Presto makeshift water-proof pants!

As it was, I layered her in all her extra clothes, hoping the cotton would prove to be as absorbent as it had been for covered wagon families, and prayed to all the gods of parenting that she'd stay dry and not have one of her famous up-the-back blowouts. I spent the remainder of the flight sniffing the air for any sign of impending diaperless doom and counting the minutes until landing.

She did stay dry, if you're wondering, but this was a nail-biting lesson in parenting:

Two is one, and one is none.

Preparation and Relaxation

Two is one, and one is none.

This old military saying also applies to parenting, which makes sense because the logistics of planning a coordinated land, air, and water strike are pretty comparable to traveling with a baby and a toddler, right?

What the saying means is pack what you think you need. Then pack one more. It's sound advice.

But take heart, because if you don't pack enough, you *will* figure it out.

The art of parenting is to over-prepare and then let it go. Over-prepare to the extent you can regarding the things that are necessities—diapers, snacks, wipes, snacks, water, adult snacks, and kid snacks. Once you've done that, relax knowing that you've done your best.

What you don't need to pack is worry. You don't get extra parenting points for how much you stress or agonize over potential negative outcomes. You actually just drain your own energy by doing this.

You can't prepare for every possibility, because sometimes life goes sideways—especially when you combine the unknowns of travel and parenting.

So over-prepare a bit. Then do your best to relax. Trust that in your moment of need, you, the super-parent that you are, will figure it out. Or someone will help you.

Or your baby will miraculously hold it.

Child Chooses

Somewhere in the recesses of my iCloud, there is a video of 2-year-old LP "packing" for a road trip to visit our extended family. In the video she stands in that bowlegged toddler way staring up at me with big blue eyes. Into an empty suitcase, she plops a baby, a book, and one sock. I ask her if she's all set. Her tiny toddler voice is confident as she tells me almost but she needs me to pack two more things for her.

"Oatmeal and eggs, Mama."

Right.

Heed this story when I suggest letting your child choose what they bring on the trip. There is an age that this isn't going to be effective (unless you enjoy gooey breakfast foods in your suitcase). But eventually, they can start packing their own entertainment bags and even help pack their suitcases.

For my daughter, the age of independently packing her entertainment bag was 4. I had left her backpack near her room the night before, intending to fill it with some last-minute toys and art supplies before we left. In the morning, she walked into the kitchen wearing that backpack and a pride-filled smile, "Mama, my bag is packed. I'm ready to go."

No way I was going to wipe away her sense of accomplishment, so I gave her a thumbs up and didn't even check the bag before we left. I only recommend not checking the bag if you're a veteran screen freed traveler or you know your kids can hang with whatever it is they choose to pack. And even then, it was risky.

When we got in the car, items began to emerge from her backpack. She had packed a Pez dispenser devoid of Pez, a bag of colored pencils and markers, the whole stack of paper from my printer tray, an empty toilet paper roll ("for artworks, Mama"), a pair of scissors (luckily we were driving, not going through TSA on that trip), a broken necklace ("it wanted to come, Mama, it's never been on a road trip before!"), her headphones for audiobooks, a small stuffed unicorn, and a pad of sticky notes. It looked like a lot of junk to me, but it was gold to her and entertained her for the whole trip.

Take Your Time

There are two approaches to kids' entertainment bags during the trip. You can give them the bag at the start. Or you can hold onto the bag and dole out items in it.

I'm more of a doler. I have found that it extends the amount of time my daughter will play with each item. Maybe your child will not like having to ask for another item or not being able to see all their options at once. You know your kiddo best, but I'll share what I did until she was 5.

When we get on the plane or before we pull out of the driveway, I give her the least stimulating item. Maybe it's a stuffed animal to snuggle or a baby doll. She may say something like, "No, I want more to play with." Then I usually cite the need for me to drive safely in traffic or to situate our bags on the plane or bus or listen to the flight attendant's instructions. Whatever gives me a plausible reason to ignore her request for a bit.

Sure enough, within a minute or so of not being given something else, she is usually singing to the baby or engaged in imaginative play with the low-stimulation item. For your child, the version of this may be a piece of blank paper and a few coloring implements, a single matchbox car, or a few magnet blocks. You likely know what low-stim items your child prefers.

Then I wait. I never offer her another item or activity until she asks.

The reason for this is that we parents tend to underestimate our children's ability and desire to play with one thing. Children have a reputation for having the attention span of fruit flies. Not only is this unfair, it's untrue. When a child is truly absorbed by something, time seems to stop for them. If you've seen a toddler squatting down to inspect a roly poly or a preschooler intent on building the tallest tower ever, you have witnessed their incredible ability to focus. In fact, as we age and become more accustomed to the instant gratification of smartphones and the Internet, I've observed children's attention spans outstripping their parents' at times.

Often, our belief about their limited attention span causes us to bombard them with options for entertainment at the first sign of boredom or waning interest. I've seen a child's gaze leave her page to stare into seemingly nothing—clearly lost in her own imaginings—and then be interrupted by a well-meaning adult saying, "All done with your drawing then?"

Even if your child has finished with an activity, it may be because he's been trained to move quickly from task to task by public school or trained by screens to crave rapidly changing stimuli.

But the human brain hasn't evolved much from our cavepeople days. It wasn't created to respond to code switching or constantly changing inputs for long periods. It's why hours of video gaming can produce a trancelike state not unlike the effect of drugs (more info on this in *Glow Kids* by Nicholas Kardaras, another excellent read).

Our brains need stillness too. We crave focus. Even when we think we don't deserve it or don't believe we can accomplish all we must if we do only one thing at a time. We are meant to use these powerful minds to solve problems with deep thinking, to create things that never existed before, to connect to our environment, and to connect to one another—all aspirations that require presence and the space to be unhurried.

When your child tells you he's ready for a new toy, book, or activity, choose the next least-stimulating one and continue on in this fashion.

If passing out items doesn't work for you, your children, or the safety of operating a moving vehicle, then I still suggest not giving them everything at once. Even when LP packed her own backpack for our trip, I stuck something up front with me where she couldn't see it. I also stash things for her in my bag even when she packs her own. Which leads me to the next hack: the elephant of surprise.

The Elephant of Surprise

"I don't want to tell Uncle Reiss we are having his birthday party. I want to do the elephant of surprise!" my daughter whispered to me as we finished wrapping his birthday gift. The elephant of surprise! Thankfully I managed to stifle my giggle. She's at an age where laughing at what she says is viewed as the highest form of betrayal.

I love the little mistakes and tweaks our children make to language as they are learning it. Maybe you're like me and you ushered some of those made-up words into the family vernacular ("basebow" for basement comes to mind for our family) and mourned the day your child mastered the correct pronunciation or phraseology.

But LP had a point: the elephant—or element, rather—of surprise is a masterful emotional tool. It's long been used by authors, screenwriters, comedians, entertainers, politicians, and anyone who wants to evoke emotions in their audience—including parents.

Surprise is a simple, yet powerful trick. On nearly every trip we've taken, I've had some new item or activity for LP that she's never seen before.

Despite how much we travel, this isn't costly, because these are usually small items. I found colorable stickers at Target once and brought a different sheet on each trip. I bought 10 different themed (horses, firehouse, airplane, dinosaur, etc.) tiny sticker books on sale at Michael's for one dollar each, and those lasted us five trips. We do toy rotation, so sometimes it's just a stuffed animal or a baby she hasn't seen in months. One time it was a set of bracelets and necklaces that I already had so we could be "twins."

The Dollar Store is a great place for small new items. Garage sales and hand-me-downs are also good sources. If you have a book lover, the library is good too (though I am way too nervous to take a library book traveling in case it gets lost). Thriftbooks.com or a local used bookstore can provide new travel books for a few dollars each.

The point is you don't have to spend a lot of money to capitalize on the surprise factor. You actually don't have to spend a lot of money on child-friendly trip entertainment at all. I can guarantee analog items are way less expensive than an iPad!

We've covered the novelty factor—never underestimate it—now let's discuss how far a solid sales pitch can go.

Sell, Sell, Sell!

Don't ever let anyone tell you parents can't sell! Half of parenting is convincing, compelling, and motivating our kids to do things that they resist simply because they can.

When it comes to the items in your "elephant of surprise," you can get more mileage, elevate the mood, use up some time, and have fun by selling it to them.

I don't just hand the surprise item to LP. I build up to it and then deliver it like a punchline.

I might pretend it's stuck in the bag and make a scene trying to heave it out. I might have her play 20 questions to guess what it is. I might have it dance or fly its way to her.

Sometimes a grand reveal falls flat, especially if you have a threenager like I did. But this too, can be fun and funny. The item can walk dejectedly back into the backpack hilariously weeping. I don't know at what age personification stops being funny, but I'm 38, and I haven't hit it yet.

If there's one thing I've learned in marketing, it's that presentation matters. You can make any small thing better by being excited about it.

Back-Up Entertainment You Don't Need to Pack

If your child is struggling with travel boredom and has run out of activities or is fed up with everything they brought, teach them to utilize their environment. What entertains a child may be far simpler than we think.

LP was 9 months old when she and I were boarding our flight to Paris. A gorgeous, silver haired flight attendant who looked straight out of a Hollywood travel romcom, caught sight of LP. "Ah," she said in her French accent, "I will be right back." She returned with four blue United Airlines cups.

Puzzled, I reached for them. Before the flight attendant could explain why she brought them, LP lunged nearly out of my arms for the cups.

I'm not exaggerating when I say those cups provided at least two hours of inflight entertainment. I stuck one over my mouth and sucked in so it stayed put. I put them on my head and LP put them on her head. She stacked them and knocked them over. She slapped an overturned cup like a tiny drum. We peered through them at one another. She put snacks into one, then the other, and so on. LP handed me a cup, then her Dad a cup, then took them back from us with the delight of a tiny pirate plunderer. Those blue cups and the flight attendant who brought them were the heroes of that eight-hour flight.

The moral? Never underestimate the power of creative play with simple materials.

I already mentioned finding the baby in the inflight safety materials. That's become a tradition for us, almost like checking on an old friend.

Introduce your child to the original screen—the window. When we fly, my daughter and I talk about how the view changes between our departure location and our destination. We report what we can see—a swimming pool, then a lake, now mountains, now mostly clouds, now the ocean. One time, I told LP that since it was such a busy day at the airport, the sky might be busy too. She spent a lot of the flight staring intently out the window, determined to see another airplane fly past.

When we drive over the mountain passes to visit family, we compete to see who can spot an animal first. We look for "dancing trees," which are just trees moving from the wind. If your road trips are in the city, look for playgrounds or school buses, their favorite restaurants, or a certain kind of car. As they get older, road trip scavenger hunt cards can provide hours of delight.

Getting a special drink or snack from the flight or train attendant can spark interest from a disgruntled tiny passenger, even when it's just the free snacks or a bubbly water.

People watching is a favorite pastime of mine and LP's, though I had to wait until she was beyond the phase of asking loud, embarrassing questions about strangers.

Is a tantrum building? Give your child some agency. Let them select whether their airplane light or fan is on or off.

The cheapest thing you can pack is your and your child's imaginations! Spending the time when they're young to teach them to use their environment means that when they're older, the screen-free, self-directed entertainment possibilities are endless!

What to Buy

I'm a list maker. Years ago, I created a Google sheet with must-have baby and early toddler items for a few of my friends who were pregnant after me to take the overwhelm out of "what do my baby and I *actually* need?"

One of my favorite things to do is to cut through the noise and clutter of the modern world to the heart of what helps families. This book is all about helping you to do the same.

I want to empower you to navigate around what society says you and your kids need and what inherited beliefs say you should feel and do. I hope you feel equipped to make clear-headed, values-based choices for you and your family. Choices that fit who you are.

So ... do you need to *buy* anything in order to create screen freedom today?

Of course not.

What you *need* is your powerful mindset, will, and a healthy dose of self-love and patience. So congrats, you have all you need already!

You might want recommendations of toys, games, and activities to take on screen freed trips and adventures. If so, I've got you.

I created a shopping list of the non-digital toys, activities, and other tools I've used or come across in my travels. It's even categorized by age. To grab this list before your next trip, visit ScreenFreedRevolution.com/look-up-resources or scan the QR code below.

While I recommend these items to make screen freed travel easier on you, I wholeheartedly believe this: You've got everything you need inside of you to do this—not only to travel with your kids without relying on devices but also to parent them into wonderful, contributing adults. There is too much money being made by a parenting industry that wants you to believe you don't have enough, you don't know enough, or you aren't capable enough. Those are lies.

You are doing an incredible job. I am proud of you. And I am proud to be doing this parenting gig alongside you.

CHAPTER 17

Snacks, Snacks, and More Snacks

I F YOU ASK EXPERIENCED SCREEN-FREE TRAVELING PARENTS OR experienced screen-friendly traveling parents for advice, both groups are going to start with snacks, bring up snacks in the middle, and end with snacks. Take it from this mama whose child experienced a gremlin-plus-water effect on one hungry road trip through a mountainous area with no places to stop for supplies—you do *not* want to run out of food.

I don't know if there's a biological reason, but there is something about being out of their natural environment that makes children's hunger take on a desperate quality. Unfed, this desperation takes the form of turbo whining, tears, high emotions, and ultimately, tantrums. If you let it go too far, they may enter "only XYZ certain food will suffice" territory. This is especially terrifying if you don't have XYZ with you. (Collective parental shudder!)

When I travel, I pack snacks as if my daughter and I are going to be lost in the woods for a week with the possibility of summiting a mountain.

She has worn her own backpack in the airport since she was about 2½, and it's usually 50/50 snacks to entertainment items. My backpack is also crammed with food plus our water bottles. I'm sure the TSA agents checking our carry-on bags expect to see a family of five passing through the metal detector and are shocked when it's just the two of us.

Remember, it's not just the plane ride you have to pack for. It's whatever meal you may be flying through. It's waiting for luggage, waiting for a rental car or catching public transit, and then traveling to your destination. Never underestimate how much hunger can happen during this time.

If you're driving, packing snacks keeps you from succumbing to crappy gas station food or expensive, time-sucking travel meals.

And by the way, the snacks aren't just for the kids. Have you tried parenting while hungry or thirsty? Unless you've ascended to some kind of saintly parenting level I have no hope of attaining, you, too, might be a little less "gentle parent" and a little more, "Be quiet right now or I might actually eat you" when hungry. The monster in the Snickers commercials is funny but not exactly the role model I want to channel for parenting.

Most importantly, you need to be your best self to not succumb to pressing the easy button—in this case, the iPad shaped one. Willpower requires fuel. So set yourself up for success with an abundance of snacks.

What Kind of Food?

My favorite parenting humor involves Instagram videos in which parents share sarcastic parenting hacks. Like "I find that if you simply give up on ever having a clean house, parenting is really quite easy. Follow me for more parenting hacks." These crack me up, because there is usually a grain (or more) of truth to them.

But this one really is a hack, albeit a simple one. Pack slow-eating snacks.

By doing this, you satiate your kid's appetite, and you create an activity. If your son rips open an individual bag of Annie's Cheddar Bunnies and dumps it into his mouth in two seconds, that snack doesn't buy much travel time.

But a cutie orange that your kiddo has to peel gives him something tactile to do *and* feeds him. (I'm always amazed at how adept toddlers are at peeling these!) These are other great options:

- Whole fruit, grapes on the vine, half of a cucumber vs. slices
- Peanut butter filled items (and plenty of liquids to wash them down of course)
- Beef jerky
- String cheese (challenge them to peel off the skinniest possible strips)

Food can be fuel and entertainment in one.

Sometimes I pack a small bento box type snack that my daughter has to assemble—think Ritz Crackers, lunch meat I've quickly chopped into smaller squares, pieces of cheese, and random fruits. She is a food experimenter, so she'll busy herself creating different combinations that I'm then forced to taste test. This happens at breakfast too, much to my chagrin. If you've never had oatmeal topped with a bite of bacon and squirted with grapefruit juice, consider yourself lucky.

Behold: Germs, Crumbs, and Thriving Anyway

I gave birth to my daughter in the winter of 2018. You may not remember, but there were a lot of stories in the news about the flu that season. It was killing an unusual amount of old people, but it was also taking down young, healthy people. It's okay if you've forgotten that particular winter—what with the worldwide pandemic we've had since then. But that flu season was burned into my brand-new-mama mind with the fire that is the biological need to protect our offspring.

So I became a bit of a germaphobe when she was born.

I kept her infant seat covered at all times when we went to restaurants, except when feeding – as if people could transmit the flu by just looking at her. I made people wash their hands like they were prepping for surgery as soon as they walked into our home. As the winter eased into spring, my concerns about the flu virus eased somewhat too.

But that experience had indelibly changed me as a mother. I became far more germ-conscious than I had been before. While I was all about her playing in the dirt, chewing on the random stick she found in the backyard, and being out in the world, anything that came to food and other humans' germs left me feeling pretty stressed.

If you also struggle with this, take care of yourself during travel.

If you're worried about germs on shared public transit (don't read the stats on this, it will not ease your fears), there are ways to mitigate that. Clorox makes little travel packs of their wipes, and you can wipe down the seats and food trays. Of course, in this post-COVID world, we all know about travel size hand sanitizer spray. Another helpful item are disposable, sticky-backed placemats. They fit perfectly on the seatback trays of most planes and trains, and they have the added benefit of being fun for children to look at. Some even feature numbers, shapes, and letters.

Another common worry for parents is about making a mess on the airplane. I always amuse myself by walking down the aisle of a mostly deboarded plane and looking at chaos left behind. Surprisingly, it's sometimes an aisle of only adults that boasts the most crumbs or debris.

If the thought of making a mess stresses you out, there are a couple options. You can pack snacks that aren't likely to make a mess like foods that don't break down to crumbs. You can spend your travel time wiping things down and contorting yourself in half bending to pick up debris.

You can also practice acceptance. Remember that from the mindset chapter? You have children. They make messes at home and at restaurants and on public transit. You know that your family isn't making unnecessary messes for the sake of someone else cleaning them up. Mess is a common side effect of being young. As for the crumbs that happen to fall in the natural course of eating—can you be like Elsa and let it go?

Planes get messy. Adults spill Starbucks drinks (and by adults, I mean me, last year, all over myself) and cocktails. Adults drop crumbs. It's great to be well-intentioned about trying not to make a mess. But don't let it stress you out or ruin your trip. The airplane cleaners are, after all, there for a reason. Be kind to yourself and your child if you give them a little something extra to clean.

CHAPTER 18

What Support Do You Need?

M Y DAUGHTER CAME BOUNCING INTO OUR HOUSE WEARING A NEW Elsa dress. Her words tumbled excitedly over one another as she tried to share every fun moment at once from her trip to Disneyland with her dad. Her joy was palpable. I reserved questions for later and enjoyed the high-energy torrent punctuated by statements of "Mama, you wouldn't believe how cool Disneyland was!" and "Mama, a huge roller coaster with loop-de-loops! Can you even imagine?!"

Amidst the excitement of the trip to the proclaimed happiness capital, she also told me about watching a movie on the airplane ride there and back. She announced with rapturous shock like I'd say to you, "And then I turned on my car and instead of driving, it flew to the supermarket!" That's because it was her first time ever watching a show on an iPad, let alone on an airplane.

My heart sank.

Her father and I separated when she was just over 2 years old. In the two years following, I had taken her on numerous travels from three-hour flights to seven-hour road trips. We'd done it all without her watching or doing anything on a screen.

Before their trip, I had asked her dad to do the same. I had given him all my best tips. I handed him a child already accustomed to travel without screens. I had implored him to not make future travel hard for me by giving her a device. It's easier to travel screen-free with a child who's never had device access than one who has had it and is now being denied.

And he had chosen differently.

I had many feelings. Even though more than a year has passed since then and she's taken another flight with him with more screen time, I still have big feelings about it.

But here's the reality: I don't need his support or alignment.

I would like it. I would like it very much, partly because it makes my life easier. Mostly because it would create consistency for our daughter between the two households. I would like to see his support show up in his actions.

But it doesn't. It won't. And that is a reality I've worked hard to accept.

The choice to be entirely screen-free, to limit screen time, or to be purposeful with the types of screen usage is individual. Even in married households, there can be variance between two parents. Screen-time choices are affected by age and generation, culture, socio-economic class, single parenthood, and a bevy of other factors.

If I, a person who has literally written this book about reducing time on screens, cannot convince my child's father—who admits that he loves the positive effects of LP being raised low-screen—to leave her off a screen for a short flight, you can bet someone in your life will not understand and may even oppose your choices regarding screens.

If we are waiting for everyone to agree with us, we'll be waiting forever.

If we are hoping to make the choice that doesn't upset, offend, or confuse anyone, we will find that option doesn't exist.

In *Reset Your Child's Brain*, Victoria Dunckley says, "All parents, without exception, must deal with the doubts and skepticism of others."

We may face doubt and skepticism and their ugly cousin, judgment.

In the limited screen families Facebook groups I'm part of, parents frequently post about the challenges of getting people around them to support and comply with their preferences. Spouses, coparents, babysitters, grandparents, teachers, neighbors, and our kids' friends' parents all have their own opinions. Whether they're rooted in science or emotion or some of both, their beliefs likely won't perfectly match ours.

We don't have to like it, but we can live without their approval. Because we have done the work to align our beliefs with our choices and our choices with our actions, we can set the necessary boundaries to protect our kids.

We don't need other people's permission or agreement. But for people we have to cooperate with, we can open healthy dialogues that facilitate understanding.

Healthy Dialogue

I encourage you to assess your why before engaging someone in a dialogue about your choices or theirs. If it's to prove a point, show them they're wrong, or defend yourself against someone who isn't listening, I suggest considering whether or not you need them "on your side." My drive to convince everyone to limit screens is strong, but it's only a productive conversation if the other person is open to it. If not, our precious energy is best spent on ourselves, our growth, and our own little circus.

However, if you need to collaborate with the person (e.g. your spouse or your kids' grandparents) in raising your children, it's helpful to be able to discuss, collaborate, and compromise on the role of screen time. I've had a lot of these conversations. Here is what has worked for me.

When a subject is potentially contentious, I recommend starting with questions. Ask them to share their perspective on screens for kids. If they are sticking with big ideas like "this is just the way the world is going," see if you can help them drill down a bit more to their personal, deeper reasons. Below are some genuine concerns parents have shared with me and suggestions for constructive responses.

Concern: "I'm afraid Carlos will be left behind or at a disadvantage if he doesn't get early enough access to devices and technology. I fell behind in math, and I feel like I never caught back up."

Response: "I can see why that would worry you. I don't want Carlos to fall behind either! Thank you for thinking of that and for sharing what happened to you. In the research I've done, I have read that children easily catch up even if they don't start with technology young. I felt really relieved when I read that. Do you have resources saying something else? Would you be open to doing some research on this together?"

Concern: "I am exhausted from taking care of kids all day, and I just want a break. Screens are how I get a break. What's the big deal?"

Response: "You work so hard and do so much for our family. I can see why you feel stretched thin. I also see how screen time feels like the most direct way to get a break. I think you deserve more support, and I'd like us to work together on solutions for that. I also read this book recently that said kids are capable of entertaining themselves from a very young age but that the more screen time they get, the less skilled they get at self-entertainment. Maybe I can help come up with some ways to let our kids strengthen that muscle so you don't feel like you have to be 'on' all the time. What do you think?"

Concern: "I love playing this video game, and I want to share it with Harper. I think she'd like it."

Response: "I love that you're excited about that! I also can't wait to play Tetris with Harper. What I have learned about screen time is that it's not all the same. Video games, in particular, affect children's brains differently than adults. Are you open to determining some boundaries together around what age Harper gets to access certain games or movies, so we know we're doing the best thing for her developing brain? I know it's hard to wait, but I think the pros outweigh the cons. Can I share with you why?"

Their answers help you better understand their feelings and the beliefs that drive their actions. As you know from the mindset chapter, awareness and acknowledgement go a long way to create connections and find common ground. You don't have to agree with their reasons to acknowledge that they exist. When someone feels seen and heard, they are much more likely to see and hear you. Not always, but much of the time.

Check In:

Who in your life has pushed back on your limited screen or screen-free choices? How do you feel about their opinions? You can use the three-part framework for acceptance to work through your reaction.

Once you've done that, can you assess if their support is necessary? If it is, can you engage them in a healthy dialogue to learn about their perspective?

If it was just a matter of making a rational case for the downsides of screens, this book would have just been the length of the next chapter. Instead, we've gone on an 18-chapter journey to explore our emotions, beliefs, and habits regarding screen time. The people around you might also need space and help to come around.

The Case Against Screen Time for Young Children

I<small>T'S TIME TO GET INTO THE RESEARCH. IT IS OVERWHELMINGLY CLEAR</small> that screen time for young children has negative outcomes that have to be weighed against the benefits. It's not just the screens themselves, but what they are displacing or preventing. We've touched on some of that in the chapters on boredom.

This chapter is not comprehensive. Screen overuse has been linked to negative outcomes in learning and school, physical ailments including obesity, sleep disruption, and increased risk of type 2 diabetes, and mental health risks including anxiety, depression, and suicide. In the following sections, I'll focus on some of the concerns around screen time for young kids, as well as the specific ways it can interfere with travel.

Use this information to inform your decisions. You can also share it with anyone you identified in the previous chapter who has doubts about how screens affect young children.

As you read this, you may encounter information you wish you'd known sooner. You may start to feel shame for choices you've made in the past. But we already know that acceptance, not shame, is the path forward. You, the devoted and brave parent who chose to pick up this book? You are here facing the truth bravely.

So blow You From the Past a kiss. They were doing their best. We are all doing our best.

Travel is About People, Not Just Places

In 2018, a survey of 20,000 people by Cigna found that Gen Z was the loneliest generation. They were even more lonely than the elderly.

Gen Z is the first to grow up only knowing a digitally connected world. (The oldest among them were 10 when the iPhone came out.) It broke my heart to read the loneliness report, yet I wasn't surprised. Z is a generation of people who are rarely technologically alone and more digitally intertwined than ever. Yet they have discovered it can't replace human connection and presence.

One of the reasons we travel is to experience new cultures. Culture isn't just different looking buildings and landscapes, new foods, and unique customs. It's the people! Traveling without engaging locals is kind of like the difference between watching a sport and playing it. You can describe the plays you watched and be really excited about it, but you didn't experience the game the same way as the players. Full engagement in travel and the people we meet along the way can gently pry us open a bit, leaving us indelibly and beautifully changed.

Whether traveling internationally or staying in our own country, there are abundant opportunities for a shared connection and for learning from others. When I reminisce over my travels, it's the conversations, shared laughter, and stories from locals that stick with me even more than the landmarks.

And I don't only mean local people at the destination. Talking to other travelers is part of the experience too. In my experience, people en route to somewhere are primed for adventure and new experiences. This makes them delightful conversationalists. Chats with other travelers, whether at a terminal, on a plane, at a hostel or hotel, or during an outing usually flow more easily than in regular life. People want to share their experiences and hear yours. At Starbucks at the Paris airport, an older couple gave me great advice on Alaskan cruises. On a ferry in Vancouver, I got the scoop on the best whale watching guide in Victoria.

Kids are incredible at making friends anywhere they go. They don't let small things like language barriers or differences in appearance keep them from building connections. They're primed to seek out and interact with other humans. But this is only possible when they are looking up at the world around them. Gaze downward and mind buried in a digital world, they will miss opportunities to connect with the people around them or to see the very place you came to explore.

This engagement isn't just important during travel. Connecting with other humans is the building block of social and relational skills.

I know I'm not the only parent who wants my child to have deep relationships and meaningful interactions with people. I also want my daughter to feel comfortable in social situations, to be able to communicate with colleagues, friends, lovers, and strangers, and to face difficult conversations with bravery and confidence. No device can teach her that. The only way to get there is through practice engaging with other humans.

LP went from an extreme separation anxiety diagnosis at 2 years old to being one of those people at 5 years old who makes friends everywhere she goes. On both legs of our last trip, she engaged other passengers in such deep conversations that they exchanged emails with me. As we deplaned ahead of them, LP hollered back, "We'll write to you!"

Developmental Skills

Let's take a step back from devices being "bad" and just look at whether they're contributing something unique. Furthermore, are they contributing to our children more than analog tools?

The answer is a complicated no.

It's undeniable that we can use technology to access information and knowledge. If your child wants to learn something, like how to speak Japanese, and you are unable to teach them due to time, knowledge, or other constraints, they might learn through an app. Before smart devices, access to that type of information was limited or nonexistent. Clearly, there's a benefit to technology expanding their realm of learning.

However, what young children (5 and under) need to learn and gain is far less knowledge-based. Instead, it's experiential.

They need to learn language and how to engage in a conversational cadence that gives and takes.

They need years of specific physical activities to develop fine motor coordination and the shoulder, arm, and finger strength to hold and move a pencil. This is the foundation of reading and writing.

They need to learn how to navigate and express their feelings through emotional regulation.

They need to interact with others to develop skills of negotiation, cooperation, collaboration, and compromise.

None of that comes from a device.

Watching people converse in a children's show will never replace the real life experience of conversation.

Swiping in games on an iPad doesn't contribute at all to the fundamentally critical muscle strength and dexterity children need to be able to write (for a deeper dive on what *does*, check out the book *Balanced and Barefoot* by Angela J. Hanscom).

The research shows us that devices cannot only *not* teach emotional regulation, screen time is actually detrimental to it. This is especially true for children.

It can be argued that games like Minecraft played with other people create opportunities for negotiation, cooperation, collaboration, and compromise. They are also gateways for strangers to gain access to your child. Play with other children is the safer pathway to such skills.

So while they're on devices children are missing out on what they need, but it's worse than that.

It's not *just* that screen time can't contribute to these fundamental building blocks of development. What's most concerning about screen time is this: it actually reduces a child's time (and desire) for the activities that do support development.

Screen time takes up space in the finite landscape of childhood that should otherwise be filled with the developmentally-fulfilling moments of real life.

We've got to relinquish the idea that just because it's new or technologically advanced or it has the word "learning" in its name, that it's better for our kids. This simply isn't true. More often, the no tech or low tech option is better for them. As I mentioned earlier in the book, the "dumber" the toy is, the more the child's brain has to work to use it. The more space there is for imagination to create from scratch. The more opportunity there is for the child to physically interact with the activity instead of passively sitting and swiping.

We can't expect children to choose the analog activity once they've had the digital one. Scribbling with a crayon on a sheet of paper instead of the vivid, instantaneous color filling in Pigment or another iPad coloring app? It's possible the child will choose the crayon (kids are naturally inclined toward the tangible), but it's not likely.

We as parents have to guard the developmentally critical real life experiences that shape our children's brains, bodies, nervous systems, and relational skills. These years are the foundation of their entire lives. Do we want them to be good at gaming—or human-ing?

If regular life is the sandbox of development, then travel is the Grand Canyon. Being in unfamiliar situations is kind of like walking on uneven ground, it requires our brains (and bodies) to practice new ways of stabilizing, of keeping upright. What a glorious time to be off screens and available to the experience.

You are traveling with your kids to take them to new places, so *be* in the new place! Limiting their screen time expands their growth opportunities. Think of the times you've come back from traveling a different person than when you left. The same is beautifully true for your children when they're given the chance to be present and engaged in the experience.

Tech Neck

Have you ever marveled at what large heads toddlers have? Apparently, that's because their brains grow the most during early years of life, reaching 90% of their adult size by age 5. To accommodate these relatively huge brains, children's heads undergo rapid growth in head height, head length, and forehead width between 1 and 6 years of age.

The average adult head weighs 11 pounds. Larger heads can top 15 pounds. That's double the weight of most newborns! These human baby-sized noggins are supported by just 7 vertebrae in the neck and about 20 muscles.

When completely upright, the head is not much of a burden; our bodies are designed to hold it there. But when we gaze down and our head tilts forward as well, it puts enormous pressure on the bones and supporting muscles. A 2014 study found that when people lean forward to look at their smartphones with their necks at a 45-degree angle, the weight of their head exerts a pressure of 60 pounds! That's the equivalent of a 9-year-old hanging off their neck (a weight some of us have actually experienced).

A person's 11-pound head can exert 60 pounds of pressure simply by tilting enough to see a phone held out at their upper chest level. Try holding your phone at chest level and gazing at it. Then compare that to where you normally hold your phone. You hold it even lower, don't you? I know I do. The normal height at which a person holds their phone massively increases the strain on their neck far past 60 pounds. Imagine the weight of tilting your head even farther to stare down at a device sitting in your lap, where devices so often end up when kids are using them.

Now, envision a head that is only *marginally* smaller, but sitting atop the tiny, undeveloped body of a toddler or young child. We wouldn't hand a toddler or preschooler a 60-pound weight, yet we allow them to exert a force greater than their own body weight on a handful of vertebrae and muscles.

Studies show an alarming rise in cervical spine issues among children of all ages. Kids are now being treated for acute neck problems that used to only plague adults. This is extra perplexing because children are born with perfect posture. So something has changed in their environment to have brought on the massive uptick in spine issues.

That something is devices.

Seventy-five percent of the world's population spends time daily hunched over handheld devices. Peering at things below us isn't entirely unheard of. Our ancestors would have looked down to tend a fire, speak to a child, write a letter, sew a shirt, lay a snare, or plant seeds. Children throughout time have bent down inspecting the world around them and doing day-to-day tasks that require a downward gaze. But they wouldn't engage in such a task for hours at a time.

The absorption factor and the prevalence of screens is the issue.

It's the way we can grab our phone to check a quick text and get caught up in other tasks, not emerging from the fog for a half hour. It's how our children have access to every kids movie ever made without having to watch at the family TV. Saturday morning cartoons can now be 5 p.m. waiting in the grocery line cartoons, 8 a.m. driving to school cartoons, first time ever flying on an airplane cartoons, or dinner out with the family cartoons—all on phones or iPads. Applications are even more immersive, designed by experts whose sole purpose is to keep us engaged with the app as long as possible.

You get the picture; the allure of devices, their constant proximity, apps that are designed to be addictive, more and more schoolwork requiring computers, and humanity's relatively new (and largely unexplored) relationship to this technology make it easy for our kids to lose hours to that hunched over position, risking damage to their neck muscles and cervical spine.

If we can't eliminate all screen time, then a small step in the right direction is teaching proper posture: holding phones up at eye level, propping iPads up and out of laps, standing desks, and laptop lifts. But we must simultaneously be ruthless about cutting out any unnecessary screen time, especially when it's in an environment (like a car ride) that doesn't enable neck-safe usage.

Cost-Benefit Analysis

Screen freedom means running a cost-benefit analysis of screens. Most likely, you'll find this will change day-to-day, even moment-by-moment. When the costs outweigh the benefits, screen freed parents say "no thanks" to screen time.

You may set some hard and fast rules, like no devices during mealtimes. You may choose to focus more on what is replacing screen time than staying within a certain number of hours.

Screen time isn't just a question of yes or no. It's about who is getting the screen time, the quantity *and* quality, the environment (e.g. screens at eye level instead of in the lap), the purpose, what's on the screen, who's around, what space it's creating, what's potentially being displaced, and so much more.

Screen freed parents do their best to take time to consider those factors and what alternatives to screen time are available. Then they choose and then—this is important—they move the heck on. They don't waste time or energy on guilt. They trust themselves to make the best decision in the moment, always with an eye to what is the ideal overall for their family. If they swing too far one way or the other, they acknowledge it, repair, and carry on. This is true screen freedom.

CHAPTER 20

You've Arrived! Bon Voyage

Dear Friend,

Here you are. A slightly different You than the one who began reading this book.

As I write this final note to you, I am picturing you and your family enjoying travel together and building memories you'll cherish forever.

May the hopes you started with on page one be realized.

I started this book with hopes too. Here they are ...

I hope you and your family travel with presence, whether to another country or a park in the next town over. I hope you let yourself sink deliciously into the journey of going and not just arriving.

I hope your children will, one day, realize all the effort you made to give them the gift of travel. Even if they don't, I hope you still acknowledge it yourself.

I hope you see that you and those tiny humans you're raising are a gift to the world, utterly irreplaceable and magical, just like the adventures you'll have together.

And I hope when travel is challenging, you think of me sitting on an airplane with an un-diapered baby on my lap silently begging her not to poop all over me.

Happy, happy travels,

Jenna Lee

Appendix

Tools in Your Toolbelt

You can find links to all the books and resources I mention throughout *Look Up!* by visiting ScreenFreedRevolution.com/look-up-resources or scanning the QR code below.

Perspective

When I wrote this book, I wanted to be sure it was informed by more than my experiences and research. So I asked for feedback from friends and people I know who have young children. I sourced their opinions in an effort to make sure that *Look Up!* would be approachable and useful for families with all kinds of relationships to screen time and devices.

These folks are all different in terms of device usage in their families and the philosophies behind their choices. Below, I've summarized their approach to technology. (When it says "device-based" that means on any device including phones, iPads, computers, etc. but *not* the family TV.)

- Commitment to no device-based usage before third grade except supervised video chatting with family, no screen time during travel, and less than 2 hours of TV/week (this is my family).
- Device-based screen time only while traveling; limit of five hours/week of TV at home.
- Two or more hours of screen time (device and TV) per child per day but only after playing outside.

- Following the World Health Organization's recommendations of no screen time other than video chatting before 2 years old and less than one hour per day after that until age 6.
- About 15 hours of screen time usage per week, some as a family and some the kids on their own devices; nearly unlimited screens during flights and road trips.
- iPads and learning games limited to weekends or when parents are working while kids are around. Movies or games allowed during travel, balanced by activity bags.
- Focus is on quality rather than on quantity; video chatting with family is unlimited, family movies on weekends; some learning apps and games; no YouTube or Internet access.

As you can see, these approaches vary quite a bit. There are as many ways to utilize and limit technology as there are families in the world. Maybe you fall somewhere in between the descriptions above. Maybe your approach before you began this book no longer aligns with your beliefs. Wherever you find yourself and your family, may you experience the liberation of conscious choice that is Screen Freedom.

About the Author

JENNA LEE DILLON IS A SOLO MAMA, 4X ENTRE-preneur, and author who founded the Screen Freed Revolution (SFR) to lead a cultural shift toward conscious screen liberation. After years of observing rising trends in screen overuse among young children through the lens of her M.A. in Education and Human Development, Jenna Lee could no longer remain a concerned bystander. Screen Freed Revolution is her rally cry. SFR helps parents identify and dispel limiting beliefs, societal programming, and misinformation to spark confidence, critical thinking, self-trust, and family habits that nourish child development.

Through private coaching, masterclasses, speaking engagements, and her popular newsletter, *Moments*, Jenna Lee shares tools to cultivate an indomitable mindset, uncover more joy, and navigate technology boundaries with purpose and peace. If she's not writing, talking about Screen Freedom on podcasts, or hopping on a plane, she can be found playing volleyball rather poorly but with great enthusiasm. She lives with her daughter and their bossy Aussie dog in Colorado.

Connect with Jenna Lee Dillon:

ScreenFreedRevolution.com

@screenfreedrevolution

@screenfreedrevolution